Sports

AN ILLUSTRATED HISTORY

Sports
An Illustrated History

David G. McComb

Oxford University Press
New York • Oxford

To Katherine, the athlete

Oxford University Press

Oxford   New York
Athens   Auckland   Bangkok   Bogotá   Buenos Aires
Calcutta   Cape Town   Chennai   Dar es Salaam   Delhi
Florence   Hong Kong   Istanbul   Karachi   Kuala Lumpur
Madrid   Melbourne   Mexico City   Mumba   Nairobi
Paris   São Paulo   Singapore   Taipei   Tokyo   Toronto   Warsaw

and associated companies in

Berlin   Ibadan

Copyright © 1998 by David G. McComb
Published by Oxford University Press, Inc.,
198 Madison Avenue, New York, New York 10016

Oxford is a registered trademark of Oxford University Press

Design: Loraine Machlin
Layout: Greg Wozney
Picture research: Martin Baldessari

Library of Congress Cataloging-in-Publication Data
McComb, David G.
    Sports : an illustrated history / David G. McComb.
       p. cm. — (Illustrated histories)
    Includes bibliographical references and index.
    ISBN 0-19-510097-2
    1. Sports—History—Juvenile literature. [1. Sports—History.]
  I. Title. II. Series
    GV571.M35   1998
    796'.09—dc21   98-15133
                    CIP

ISBN 0-19-510097-2 (trade edition)

9 8 7 6 5 4 3 2 1

Printed in Hong Kong
on acid-free paper

On the cover: Baseball game in 1896

Frontispiece: English soccer player Frank Swift in 1949

Title page: Young sports fans at a 1942 Detroit Tigers game

Contents

Preface

Sports history is an emotional subject. Fans argue endlessly about great plays, the athletes, rules, and team qualities. With the same set of facts, sports enthusiasts can come to different conclusions. Seemingly, there is no final word on a subject, and everyone has an opinion. Anyone who reads about great sports events should understand how easy it is to get into an argument. This book tries to steer a course toward the mainstream of historical opinion—but, given the nature of the subject, there is always room for disagreement. That, of course, is part of the fun in the subject of sports.

There are only a few books about the global development of sports, but many about special topics. This volume draws on the work of other authors and could not have been written without their information. The bibliography indicates the great efforts of such scholars. It is impossible, of course, to construct a narrative world history that touches on every sport. Fortunately, the recent *Encyclopedia of World Sport,* edited by David Levinson and Karen Christensen, provides descriptions of 300 sports around the world. Their articles are a good place to start for a reader looking for information about a particular activity. Also, it is impossible to investigate all of the rules of the various sports. For such detail, a reader can refer to Graeme Wright's *Rand McNally Illustrated Dictionary of Sports,* and the Diagram Group's *Rules of the Game.*

In organizing this volume, I have followed the lead of world historians, who often arrange their topics around civilizations and long time periods. Thus I follow sports development in Mesoamerica, Asia, Africa, the Middle East, and ancient Greece and Rome. From there, the book generally focuses on the evolution of sports in Western civilization, including the United States. Woven into the fabric of the narrative are comments about the origins of various sports, the athletes, rules, the role of women and minorities, technology, geographic influences, economics, and the importance of politics. For a true sports fan, there can never be enough information about the sporting games that humans like to play. However, the information contained in this book offers a great starting place for anyone who is interested in the global development of sports.

Introduction: What Is Sport?

It began on a cool, gray morning that softened the features of Santa Monica College in southern California. On August 5, 1984, 50 women from around the world gathered on the campus to start the Olympic marathon. The American champion, Joan Benoit, felt ready. A mere two weeks before the qualifying trials, she had undergone arthroscopic surgery on her right knee to remove a fibrous mass that was blocking movement in the joint. The endoscope used in the operation required only a small incision and allowed the doctor to see inside her knee. Benoit recovered quickly, won the trials, and resumed training. Now, three months later, she faced the world's best female athletes in the first marathon for women in the history of the Olympic games.

The race was a milestone in the struggle of women to express their athletic nature. The struggle was a part of a larger quest for equal opportunity in jobs, politics, and society. The marathon was proof that women, like men, could condition their bodies to run long distances. Some women had already run such distances—Kathrine Switzer secretly entered the Boston Marathon in 1967 and finished the race in spite of the outrage of Jock Semple, the meet registrar, who tried to run her off the course. The Olympic marathon event demonstrated once again the most important purpose of sport—to reveal the human spirit through physical excellence.

Born in 1957 in Portland, Maine, Benoit grew up as a fiercely competitive youngster who ran, skied, and played field hockey. In college, running became her most important sport, and she won the Boston Marathon in 1979 and 1983 with record-breaking times. She often trained alone, logging distances of more than 100 miles per week through the Maine countryside. "The scenery changes every day, even on my most familiar loops," she wrote in her autobiography, *Running Tide*. "I watch the progress of the seasons in the colors of grass and trees; I note the additions of baby cows and chickens on nearby farms; I welcome the great blue herons to the cove; and I try to run in the first snowstorm."

She developed an efficient, machinelike stride that she monitored closely during a race.

> It's as if I'm an inventor; I created this body and now I'm watching it work. Any glitches in the moving parts? (No.) Are the pumps and valves leaking? (No.) Is there too much stress anywhere? (Not yet.) The invention can be monitored for just so long before the creator either begins to trust it or watches it break down. There's a point in every race, and it's different in each, where I realize that my body is either going to make it to the end in fine style or be in trouble. Once that point is passed I start making decisions to account for the condition of the machine.

In Los Angeles, wearing a white baseball cap over her close-cropped dark hair, Benoit

At age 27, Joan Benoit from the United States won the gold medal in the first-ever Olympic marathon for women in 1985.

broke from the pack of runners at the three-mile mark. With grim determination she relentlessly widened the gap mile by mile. The sun had broken through, the sky lightened, and on national television she appeared as a small, lone figure moving at her own pace, running on and on through streets cleared of traffic and across the empty freeway bridges toward the Olympic stadium. The machine was running smoothly and the spectators at the Los Angeles Coliseum, where the race ended, watched her progress on huge television screens as she came closer. She entered the dark tunnel leading into the arena and listened to the echo of her own muffled footfalls.

As Benoit emerged into the pale sunlight of the Coliseum's empty track the waiting crowd erupted with deafening noise. Her mother later remarked that her daughter "looked like a little gray mouse skittering out of a hole." Still alone, a minute and a half ahead of second-place Grete Waitz of Norway, she circled the track, waved her hat to the roaring fans, and crossed the finish line with a time of 2:24:52 (two hours, twenty-four minutes, and fifty-two seconds). This time, being the first, set the record for the event, and the ecstatic, smiling American runner trotted a victory lap carrying the flag of the United States.

This story of an outstanding athletic victory offers some answers to a surprisingly difficult question—what is sport and what is its importance? *Sports* is a word that everyone knows and uses. There are sports pages in newspapers, sports magazines, sports television channels, and sports segments of news broadcasts where the word is used repeatedly. Of course, everyone knows what this word means—or do they? Is fishing a sport? What about playing checkers? Or throwing a flying disc for a dog? Or lifting weights at a gym three times per week? Is there a difference between going to the local swimming pool in the summer

to splash around for an hour with friends, and going there to swim 20,000 yards per day under the supervision of a coach?

The *American Heritage Dictionary* offers a pithy definition: sport is "an activity involving physical exertion and skill that is governed by a set of rules or customs and often undertaken competitively." The important elements in the definition are physical activity and skill, rules and competition. In the example of Joan Benoit, the physical exertion and the presence of competition were apparent. There were also rules. For example, the distance of the marathon was precisely 26 miles 385 yards; runners had to stay on course with no shortcuts; there was a division of the sexes; there was an exact starting time; each nation was allowed three entries.

These three elements of physical prowess, rules, and competition seem to be particularly significant and can be used for a working definition of sport throughout human history. This eliminates games, such as checkers, in which no physical exertion is required, and leaves out recreational activities, such as playing catch, because they lack competition. Even with this definition, the line between sports and games, as well as between sports and recreation, can be unclear and blurred at times. Fishing, for example, is considered a recreation, but what if there is a fishing contest with people trying to catch the biggest fish? Under these circumstances does fishing become a competitive sport? *Sports* is thus almost too general a term. Perhaps the word *athletics* comes closer to the subject of this book. An athlete is defined as someone who is a trained competitor in a physical activity. In this book, however, when the word *sports* or even *game* appears, it is used in the sense of "athletics."

One of the best scholars in sports history, Allen Guttmann of Amherst College, offers a more complicated definition. He com-

pared the characteristics of modern sports to those of earlier days. Guttmann believes that unlike earlier periods, sports of the present time show little relation to religion, emphasize the same rules for everyone, are typically governed by national or international organizations, have developed distinct identities and specialties, and keep track of records that are expressed in numbers. Joan Benoit's marathon reflects these characteristics: there was no official linkage to a religion; everyone in the race ran by the same rules; the International Olympic Committee governed the Los Angeles games; all competitors were involved in an event for which they had specially trained; and there was concern for a timed record.

Guttmann has also considered the importance of crowds and technology. These elements are a part of the sports scene—Benoit finished her race at the Los Angeles Coliseum before a roaring crowd and an interested television audience. In simpler form many of Guttmann's modern characteristics show up in past eras. His suggestions, nonetheless, sharpen the definition and help to answer the question, What is sport?

The meaning and purpose of sport in human history is also difficult to determine. As an athlete, Roger Bannister, the great English miler who first ran a mile in less than four minutes, said, "We run, not because we think it is doing us good, but because we enjoy it and cannot help ourselves. It also does us good because it helps us to do other things better. It gives a man the chance to bring out power that might otherwise remain locked away inside himself." But does the existence of sport mean anything for a society? Bill Russell, a star professional basketball player of the Boston Celtics of the 1960s, commented in his autobiography, *Second Wind*:

> As I see it, the world of sports is in very fine company, with a fine heritage. It is one of the Big Four. Only four kinds

of events—politics, religion, the arts and sports—have been able to draw consistently large crowds of paying customers throughout history. That must mean something.

People often assume that sports reveal the character of the society in which they are played. The most famous expression of this sentiment comes from scholar Jacques Barzun. "Whoever wants to know the heart and mind of America," he wrote in his 1954 book *God's Country and Mine*, "had better learn baseball, the rules and realities of the game—and do it by watching first some high-school or small-town teams."

Clichés always demand caution, however. Barzun wrote about baseball in 1954. His statement may have been true at the time, yet might not apply to the 1990s, when other sports such as professional football and basketball have attracted similar popular interest. Could it also be said that baseball reflects the societal values of Cuba or Japan, where the American game is also very popular? Sports, nonetheless, are a part of a local culture and cannot be dismissed. There is a reason for their presence, even if transplanted, and they do say something about the character of a society and its past. In other words, sports are historical artifacts and a part of social history.

There is, however, more to say about the meaning of sports. Modern athletics are significant as entertainment and fashion. They also have important local economic effects. They generate business (and thus employment) and influence city politics and finances because of the huge public investments that are needed for the construction of stadiums and sports centers. Beyond that, sports provide a certain unity for people. Fans rally behind their team, talk about last Sunday's game, read the sports pages, place bets, find heroes and goats, mourn their losses, and become angry when their team moves to another city. In short,

The Boston Celtics take a time out under the direction of coach and player Bill Russell (center). Banners of Celtics' past championship glories hang from overhead.

heroes and teams give an identity to the hometown and provide people with a topic of conversation to break the ice with one another and around which they can rally as members of a city, state, or nation. "Sports and music have become the universal languages," says Philip H. Knight, the chief executive officer of Nike, Inc., the sports clothing company.

Sports terms, moreover, appear in everyday language as metaphors, a phrase or word taken from one aspect of life and applied to another. After one of the famous television debates between Presidential candidates John F. Kennedy and Richard M. Nixon in 1960, for example, an aide told Kennedy that Nixon "never laid a glove on you." This was a reference to boxing and meant that Kennedy had scored an easy triumph. Sports metaphors such as "level playing field," "from the word 'go,'" "saved by the bell," "strike out," "turning point," and "on target" are used frequently. In 1984 Governor Lawton Chiles of Florida prescribed a "game plan" for Presidential candidate Walter Mondale in his political campaign against incumbent Ronald Reagan. "It's like a football game," Chiles said. "Mondale can't get the ball back with one big play. But the American people love a horse race. I would advise him not to knock Reagan out."

Meaning can also be found in the "beauty" of sports. The manner in which an athlete performs can appeal to what is valued in life. Joan Benoit's victory was a combination of hard work, determination, and correct form in running. It was also a triumph for women, in general, who had been closed out of athletics and other endeavors for so long. She proved that women could train well and run lengthy distances. Traffic stopped in Los Angeles to give her room to perform. Her triumph was an inspiration: she ran well; Americans were justifiably proud of her. Because athletic performance can appeal to the senses and thrill the observer, sport represents a distinct kind of performing art, like a play or symphony concert. Considered as one of the arts, sports at their best can help explain what it means to be human and inspire people to reach for fulfillment of their greatest potential. This is the fundamental meaning of sports.

Chapter 1

The World of Traditional Sport and Early Civilizations

Humans evolved into their modern form about 30,000 years ago. Since then, with better diets, medicine, and safety, people have managed to grow larger in size and live a longer time. Other than that, the physical elements have remained constant—humans are born with the same basic parts, learn to crawl, walk, grow, speak, and otherwise grow up. As they develop, humans seem to experience pleasure in the movement of their bodies. (A considerable amount of research has been published on the subject of play in animals and humans.) Children run, chase, tumble, and prance. The wall paintings of prehistoric humans, the earliest art, show running and dancing scenes. Thus what Roger Bannister experienced as a youth is probably a common human experience and the source of interest in sports.

In his book, *First Four Minutes*, Bannister recalled a moment of physical rapture on a beach when he was growing up:

In this supreme moment I leapt in sheer joy. I was startled, and frightened, by the tremendous excitement that so few steps could create. I glanced round uneasily to see if anyone was watching. A few more steps—self-consciously now and firmly gripping the original excitement. The earth seemed almost to move with me. I was running now, and a fresh rhythm entered my body. No longer conscious of my movement I discovered a new unity with nature. I had found a new source of power and beauty, a source I never dreamt existed. From intense moments like this, love of running can grow.

This happiness of movement remained with him from his youth into a later era of training and racing. Running is a likely candidate for the first official sport. At least, it was the first event selected by the Greeks for the ancient Olympic games that were said to have begun in 776 B.C.

Traditional sports, those that develop in a particular place or region, usually have distant origins that reach far into the past. The inborn joy of movement may have had something to do with their beginnings, but survival was also important. Those who could hunt and fight the best were the people who lived. Contests based on combat skills or hunting, therefore, were common, and spear throwing could have

Games at this ancient ball court at Chichén Itzá in Mexico were played with a rubber ball and stone hoops. They may have resembled basketball—except that they might have ended with a sacrifice to the gods.

Roger Bannister: The Four-Minute Barrier

Born in 1929, Roger Bannister grew up running away from World War II bombs and local bullies in Bath, England. He was tall, thin, and fast and not particularly good at other sports such as cricket or rugby. Instead, Bannister found satisfaction on the track. He took up serious training at Oxford University, where he enrolled in 1946 to prepare for a career in medicine. Running, he thought, was a sport for anyone with enough determination. During a surprise victory in the mile over runners from Cambridge University in 1947, he felt an overwhelming "intensity of living" and "discovered my gift for running." Over the next several years, Bannister gradually lowered his time for the mile. In July 1950 it was 4:13.0; by April 1951 it was 4:08.3.

After placing fourth in the 1,500-meter race at the 1952 Olympics, Bannister planned an assault on the four-minute barrier in the mile. It was not an impossible goal, but no one had yet managed to run that fast. The four-minute mile was as much a psychological obstacle as a physical one. From late 1953 to early 1954, John Landy of Australia won six races, all with times less than 4:03, but he could not break four minutes. "It's a brick wall," he lamented. Other runners, however, such as the American Wes Santee, were nearing the goal. Bannister himself ran a mile in 4:02.0 in June 1953.

Bannister figured that beyond good conditioning, success required four elements: a good track, no wind, warm weather, and an even pace. As it turned out, he found a good track at Oxford for an official race, but the weather was blustery on May 6, 1954. Nonetheless, he sharpened the spikes on his track shoes on a grindstone at a hospital laboratory in preparation. A passerby commented discouragingly, "You don't really think that's going to make any difference, do you?" Two friends, fellow runners Chris Chataway and Chris Brasher, agreed to help pace him through the mile, and the race started during a drop in the wind in the late afternoon. The distance was four times around the track.

After a false start, the gun fired again and Brasher led the way, with Bannister close behind. Brasher dropped off and Chataway took the lead after two laps, setting a world record pace, with Bannister following. At three-quarters of a mile, Bannister moved into first place. He was on world record pace, and the spectators were roaring. He remembered, "I had a moment of mixed joy and anguish, when my mind took over. It raced well ahead of my body and drew my body compellingly forward. I felt that the moment of a lifetime had come. There was no pain, only a great unity of movement and aim. The world seemed to stand still, or did not exist. The only reality was the next two hundred yards of track under my feet."

Bannister crossed the tape at the finish line in exhaustion, nearly unconscious. Supported by friends he heard the announcer say, "Result of one mile . . . time, three minutes . . . ." And the roar of the crowd overwhelmed the sound of the loud speaker. The time was 3:59.4. The wall had been broken, the barrier was down. Forty-six days later, John Landy ran 3:58.0. At the Empire games in Vancouver in August, Bannister beat Landy. Both of them ran the race in less than four minutes, with Bannister posting a time of 3:58.8. The record in the mile has been lowered 17 times since Bannister's great effort in 1954. The current record was set by Noureddine Morcalli of Algeria in 1993 at 3:44.39.

Roger Bannister hits the tape on May 6, 1954, the day he became the first man to run the mile in less than four minutes. His time on that day was 3:59.4.

been one of the earliest competitions. In addition, at a time when priests were powerful and supernatural forces were used to explain the mysterious changes of nature, religion often intermixed with sports. Games and contests became a part of the worship of gods or goddesses. Environment, too, could be an influence, such as the development of boat racing in places with a lot of water.

As civilizations developed out of cities, nations, and empires, sports and recreation became more complex and less tied to the needs of religion and survival. As with other aspects of culture, sports changed. Traditional sports, however, often provided the basis for the athletic contests of civilizations, and these sports were spread throughout their empires. An example of this process can be found in the Mesoamerican civilization of Mexico and Central America.

Around 200 B.C. in the central valley of Mexico, a complex culture arose that was based on trade in obsidian, a hard black stone used for tools and art. Nearby obsidian mines brought wealth to the Teotihuacano people, who built a city north of where Mexico City is now. Large pyramids, bright frescoes, a ceremonial plaza, a long thoroughfare now called Avenue of the Dead, and 100 palaces for priests dominated the city. There is evidence of the ritual sacrifice of human beings. For unknown reasons decay of the culture set in, and in 650 A.D. the city was burned and looted by enemies from the north. Satellite towns remained, however, and at Tajin on the coast near the Gulf of Mexico the dramatic pyramid architecture of Teotihuacan was repeated.

At Tajin, however, there was something else. No fewer than seven ball courts with high stone walls, shaped like the letter "I," were used to play a game called "ollama." Such open-air courts have been found also among the ruins of the Maya and Aztec cities, which replaced the Tajin civilization later in Mesoamerican civilization. No rule book remains, and there are only a few Spanish descriptions of the game. Apparently, two teams, using a seven- to eight-inch-diameter hard rubber ball, played against each other. The object was to keep the ball away from opponents and to hit it with hip or thigh through a vertical stone ring mounted high on the wall of the court. Neither hands nor feet could be used to strike the ball.

Although court sizes varied, the contests were played with enthusiasm, and sometimes money, land, and even lives were bet on the outcome. The game also had religious overtones associated with the mythology of the sun and moon. Carved stone decorations at the courts indicate that players might have been executed at the end of the game. There is disagreement about who was killed, however. Was it the loser, or was it the winner? We would normally think that it was the loser. But, if a worthy person was to be sacrificed to the gods, it might have been the winner. In the

This pyramid was built by the Teotihuacano people to honor their ancient deity and legendary ruler, Quetzalcoatl, who is credited with the discovery of maize, the arts, science, and the calendar.

Choctaw tribesmen prepare to play "baggataway" (meaning "little brother of war") as part of training for hunting and warfare.

Mayan religious myth, the ball game is intricately involved with the creation of human beings. The Spanish, who conquered Mexico in the years 1619–21, ended the game. They considered it barbaric.

Ball games with less deadly consequences were played in the forests of North America. Here, Algonquin and Iroquois tribespeople organized two- to three-day games as part of their training for hunting and war. Using trees several miles apart as goals, large groups of male and female Indians, using a branched stick with webbing, tried to score with a wooden or deerskin ball. They called the game "baggataway," meaning "little brother of war." The game was also an expression of thanksgiving and played during religious ceremonies. Early French Jesuit missionaries supposedly gave it the name "lacrosse" because the sticks reminded them of a French bishop's staff, or crosier, called *la crosse*. The same word was used by the French to describe a stick used for field hockey.

On June 4, 1763, hundreds of Sauk and Ojibwa Indians used lacrosse to capture Fort Michilimackinac in northern Michigan, as part of Pontiac's Conspiracy. The event began when Indians staged a game, supposedly in celebration of King George's birthday, outside the closed gates of the fort. When the unsuspecting British soldiers opened the doors in order to view the sport, the Indians threw down their lacrosse sticks, pulled out hidden tomahawks, and charged into the fortress. The surprise worked, the defenders were slaughtered, and the fortress fell. Although the British lost the fort, they quickly suppressed the rebellion.

Lacrosse has lasted to the present time—the first club formed in Montreal in 1839. W. George Beers of Montreal wrote the first set of accepted rules in 1867. They were roughly similar to those of field hockey. The game was Canada's most popular sport around 1900, but it lost players and appeal during World War I. Afterward interest in lacrosse partially revived, and the game is now played by both men and women, particularly in the colleges of eastern North America.

Across the Pacific Ocean, China dominated Asian civilization and traditional culture. Japan, Korea, and Vietnam were outlying recipients of Chinese culture. From the 3rd century B.C. to the 12th century A.D., China was ruled by emperors whose families reigned in dynasties lasting hundreds of years. Control of the country was centralized and a vast bureaucracy carried out the desire of the emperor, including the sporting activity.

Marco Polo, a merchant and traveler from Venice, described a hunting expedition of Kublai Khan, who completed the Mongol invasion of China in 1279. On vacation in March 1275, the Great Khan left his capital at what is now Beijing and marched toward the Pacific Ocean with elephants, horses, hunting dogs, various officers, family, members of the court, and 10,000 falconers. Competing with their birds of prey, the emperor and his followers captured herons, swans, storks, and other game. People living in the area were forbidden to kill deer, rabbits, or large birds during the months from March to October to ensure the success of the Khan's hunting trips.

The Yuan Dynasty (1279–1368), founded by Kublai Khan, also sponsored 83-kilometer runs (about 51.5 miles) that took six hours to complete. A throne was placed at the finish line so that the ruler could enjoy the triumph of the athletes as they crossed the line. At the finish the runners bowed their heads to the ground and shouted, "May your majesty live 10,000 years." The winner was awarded a bar of silver.

Other sports from an earlier period continued at this time. Cuju, a game similar to soccer, was played by teams of both men and women as a form of recreation. It was also used for military training and underwent a series of changes. Cuju was 2,500 years old, and during the T'ang Dynasty (618–906) the ball stuffed with hair was replaced with one of leather inflated with air. Goalposts replaced holes in walls as targets. Another ball game migrated to Japan where it was called kemari. It was played by people forming a circle and kicking a small deerskin ball. The object was to keep the ball in the air, much like the modern game of hackysack. Over time emphasis was on style and etiquette, not on who allowed the ball to drop. A sport like polo, moreover, which dated from the 3rd century A.D., was played in China, and court women participated with their own version using donkeys instead of horses. Soldiers and men wishing to join the government had to demonstrate skill as horsemen and archers. From galloping horses, soldiers shot their arrows at wooden rabbits and willow twigs. When a twig was severed the soldiers tried to catch it before it dropped to the ground.

Two types of unarmed combat also evolved in China, but the origins are obscured by legend. T'ai chi ch'uan, the soft form, supposedly, was created in the 6th century A.D. by the Taoist religious master Chang San-Feng. He was inspired after watching a patient snake defeat a hopping, chirping crane. Using evasive, flowing movements the snake avoided the bird until it fell exhausted. Chang taught his followers to utilize their inner energy (chi) to defeat opponents without touching them. Today t'ai chi, with its gentle, flowing movements is used mainly as a form of exercise.

While studying in China in 1983–84, Mark Salzman, an American who practiced martial arts, observed a soft-form master who went through a routine of fluid twists and kicks. When challenged, Salzman was unable to hold him. In his book *Iron and Silk* Salzman wrote, "I reached out and grabbed his arms, but with a twist of his hips and shoulders he was free. Again and again I tried to hold him still, but no matter how much strength I used he managed to wriggle free without much difficulty."

In Japan in 1882 Jigoro Kano (1860–1938) used what he called the "way of gentleness" as a basis for judo. The force of another's attack was diverted with proper leverage to throw the aggressor to the ground. Kano's emphasis was on graceful movement and technique that could overcome strength and stop an attacker. Judo became a competitive sport in Japan after World War II; the International Judo Federation formed in 1951.

The hard form, shaolin ch'uan, supposedly began at the same time as t'ai chi in north-central China. Ta Mo, a Buddhist leader, wanted to give his gentle monks a means to protect themselves from abuse. The technique involved a period of long training to learn to strike at various nerve centers with toughened hands and feet. Salzman once met a hard master known as "Iron Fist" who toughened his right hand by striking an iron plate more than 1,000 times a day. The monks traditionally insisted on rigid discipline so that this power to injure would not be misused. Errant students, allegedly, were killed by the priests who withheld a few tricks for that purpose.

On the Japanese island of Okinawa the hard form developed into karate (meaning "empty hand") with emphasis on striking an opponent with the edge of the hand. In Korea the form became tae kwon do, which featured whirling, circular kicks. In the paintings inside the Silla tombs of Korea, which date from the time of Christ, there is evidence of this unarmed combat. The technique was taught to select young men along with a code of behavior that insisted on loyalty to country, parents, and friends. It also forbade retreat in battle or making an unjust kill. Tae kwon do was partially forgotten in the 17th century, but revived as secret training to resist the Japanese occupation of Korea in the first half of the 20th century. After the first modern school of tae kwon do opened in Seoul, Korea, in 1945, many variations emerged, and a world federation for competition formed in 1973. It was presented as a demonstration sport at the 1988 Olympics at Seoul.

Although wrestling can be found as a traditional sport throughout the world, the Japanese developed a unique type, sumo. According to legend it dates back to 23 B.C., but it apparently gained its popularity in the early 1700s among the samurai warriors, the skilled swordsmen of the islands. Much about the sport, seemingly, remains unchanged, but many of the traditional ritual aspects were reintroduced in the 19th century. There are no weight classes and current wrestlers weigh as much as 450 pounds. They fight, one-on-one, in a 12-foot-diameter ring of sand and clay with the purpose of throwing or driving an opponent out of the ring.

It is a sport for large men with huge stomachs, which give them the advantage of a low center of gravity. Before the match, the glaring, puffing athletes dressed in loincloths

The Yuan dynasty of China established by Kublai Khan, a 13th-century B.C. emperor, sponsored 50-mile races that took more than six hours. A throne was placed at the finish line so that the ruler could enjoy the triumph of the athletes as they crossed the line.

Japanese Sumo wrestling dates back to 23 B.C. These two 400-pound wrestlers compete in Tokyo, 1952. At this point, Kagamisato (left) is pushing Yoshibayam out of the ring to win the match.

clap their hands to awaken the gods, throw salt on the ring to purify the ground, and stamp their bare feet to crush evil. At a signal from a referee who dresses in 14th-century costume, the two contestants charge each other, hands in front and knuckles down for a quick, explosive collision. With its throws, lifts, grunts, trips, shoves, and pulls the match is over in moments. The champions, known as *yokozunas*, enjoy life as popular heroes, live at training quarters, and are waited on by younger, less-skilled wrestlers. The position of *yokozuna* was created in 1890, a period of intense modernization, by the leaders of sumo wrestling as a symbol of the best in Japanese culture. A *yokozuna* keeps his position for life, but when he begins to lose, he is expected to gracefully retire.

During the treaty negotiations to open the ports of Japan to outside trade in 1854, Commodore Matthew Perry and his men were entertained with an exhibition of Japanese wrestling. The Americans were approached on the beach by 25 nearly naked, massive men. They appeared to be just mounds of fat with eyes barely visible in bloated heads with no necks. Invited to feel the muscles, the commodore passed his hand over folds of flab similar to a dewlap, the dangling skin on the throat of an ox. But the wrestlers were surprisingly strong and carried 100-pound sacks of rice two at a time. One of the wrestlers carried a sack with his teeth; another turned somersaults while holding a sack. After a demonstration of sumo wrestling, with its ritual and brute force, the Americans proudly showed off their model telegraph and railroad.

From the samurai also came the sport of kendo (meaning "sword path"). In train-ing, warriors used bamboo staves as substitutes for their razor-sharp swords. As early as 400 A.D., the men, shouting as they struck, practiced cutting and slicing blows to the eight major target areas of the body. Their practice was for deadly purpose, however, because samurai were subject to challenge, like gunfighters of the Old West in America. Musashi Miyamoto (1584–1645), for example, won 60 duels, including a bloody fight on a beach against the man who supposedly had killed his father. The samurai class went out of existence in the last part of the 19th century, but kendo endured as a sport with little change in equipment and costume. It was useful for modern police training. In 1928 a Kendo Association was established in Tokyo. American occupation officials banned the sport immediately after World War II, but

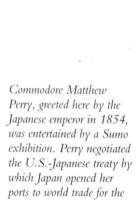

Commodore Matthew Perry, greeted here by the Japanese emperor in 1854, was entertained by a Sumo exhibition. Perry negotiated the U.S.-Japanese treaty by which Japan opened her ports to world trade for the first time.

Practicing kata, a basic kendo technique, with his instructor (right) is Lt. Col. Harold D. Parker of the U.S. Army in 1962. Though outlawed in the U.S. after World War II, kendo was revived in 1952.

in 1952 it revived with the establishment of the All Japan Kendo Federation.

Compared to East Asian civilization, Indian civilization offers less information about traditional sports. Covering the subcontinent, Indian civilization embraced what are now the countries of Pakistan, India, and Bangladesh. A Chinese traveler in the 7th century B.C. noted archery, ball games, chariot driving, sword fighting, elephant riding, and swimming as activities. In the folk literature, in addition, there is some evidence of sports activity. In the Sanskrit epic *Ramayana,* the hero Rama obtains permission to marry Princess Sita in a contest to bend the bow of the god Siva. The bow was so large that it took an eight-wheeled wagon to carry it. Nonetheless, Rama was strong enough not only to bend the bow, but also to break it. In the other great Indian epic poem, the *Mahabharata,* which contains the teachings of the god Krishna, there is mention of archery, sword, and wrestling contests.

In southern India, Tamil herdsmen fought barehanded with bulls to prove their manhood. Entering an arena, they wrestled a bull in an attempt to master it, as an American cowboy might try to throw a steer to the ground by grasping it about the horns. Women watching from the fences chose their husbands from the survivors. An early poem describing a bull with bloody human entrails hanging on its horns indicated that the bull sometimes won the contest. There is little evidence, however, in Indian history of sports development beyond these traditional activities.

In the Middle East, the Mesopotamian civilization flourished in the region of the Tigris and Euphrates river valleys from 3500–539 B.C. Impressive cities and palaces ruled by kings and priests with an ambition for conquest and invasion mark the history of the civilization. Individuals counted for little and human subjects were unimportant in art. Nakedness was considered a humiliation. This was a great contrast to the Greek and Egyptian civilizations of the same time, which glorified the human body. Herodotus, the wandering Greek historian of the 5th century B.C., wrote that both men and women of the Middle East thought it shameful to appear nude. This was an attitude that has seemingly endured to the present time in the culture of the region. For sports this was important, because without a willingness to shed or adjust clothing so the body can move freely, it can be difficult to attain athletic excellence.

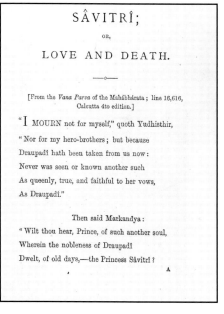

*A section of the great
Indian epic poem*
Mahabharata, *which
mentions sports including
archery, wrestling, and
sword contests.*

Kings were considered divine in Mesopotamia, and physical prowess was considered symbolic of their power. The civilization developed horse-drawn war chariots, and royal hunting scenes with chariots are found carved into the walls of the ancient cities. The palace at Nimrud, for example, portrayed King Ashurnasirpal II, an Assyrian monarch who ruled from 883 to 859 B.C., killing lions with a bow while soldiers with shields forced the lion toward the king's chariot. A temple wall at Nineveh, furthermore, portrayed a staged lion hunt of King Ashurbanipal, who reigned from 668 to 626 B.C. With bow and arrow, the king killed lions released from cages. He shot from behind a warrior's protective shield while spectators and chariots stood nearby. Scattered archaeological evidence also shows wrestling, swimming, and boxing scenes. A tablet from 1200 B.C. described foot races at new year's festivals.

The oldest narrative poem of any culture, the *Epic of Gilgamesh*, which dates from the Akkadian period of 2300 B.C., mentions a sporting contest. The epic concerns the search for immortality by a human being born of a goddess. Gilgamesh, the hero, meets his best friend through a wrestling match. "The two grappled in combat,

and struggled and lowed and roared like two wild bulls. They destroyed the pillar of the door and the wall shook. . . . But when Gilgamesh, bracing his foot on the floor, bent over and threw Enkidu, the heat of his fury cooled and he turned away to leave." The defeated man recognized the superiority of Gilgamesh, and the two became companions for life. The poem involved one of the oldest of sports, wrestling, and in the ancient Babylonian calendar "Gilgamesh's month" became a time designated for wrestling competitions.

Sports, however, were generally not important in Mesopotamian life, nor in the Middle East at later periods. After Rome conquered the area, officials in 174 B.C. built a gymnasium for Greek sports at Jerusalem, and later, under the governor Herod (37 B.C.–4 A.D.), a stadium for gladiator fighting and chariot racing. According to the books of Maccabees, which contain early Jewish history in the century before Christ, young Hebrew men, trying to impress the conqueror, underwent surgery to disguise their prior circumcision so that they could compete nude. Most of the Jewish community, however, rejected sports as a part of a hated foreign culture. This rejection continued in the Middle East until after World War II.

Under Islamic (Muslim) rule, athletic development likewise suffered. Muhammad (570–632), the founder of Islamic civilization, recommended running, wrestling, archery, spear play, horseback riding, swimming, and tumbling. These activities were for military training or relaxation, however, and were not to take precedence over religious duty. Religious obligations, ac-

*This tablet dates from
2300 B.C. and contains the*
Epic of Gilgamesh, *the
oldest narrative poem of any
culture. Gilgamesh met his
best friend through a wrestling
match.*

cording to Muhammad, included fasting with no food or water allowed in daylight during the lunar month of Ramadan. The commandment for fasting is still a part of the religion now embraced by more than 1 billion people. This lack of nutrition, obviously, is not healthy for athletes.

Islam spread through the Middle East, southern Europe, North Africa, and eastward into India. Much of the area was desert country of high heat where outdoor exercise was uncomfortable, if not dangerous. Fatigue and perspiration were to be avoided. Where the religion took root in North Africa, Muslims devalued traditional sports events as pagan celebrations at which spectators drank beer. Alcoholic beverages were forbidden to Muslims.

Moreover, according to Islamic custom, women were kept veiled and secluded.

Nakedness was considered wrong, and even men could not expose their knees. Under such circumstances, stripping down for athletic activity was immoral. In addition, because women were kept at home they had little opportunity for athletic training. Even today in the Muslim nation of Iran, for example, women cannot compete in swimming, track, basketball, or volleyball because of immodest dress. In an attempt to qualify for the 1996 Olympic kayak events, Iranian women trained while wearing *chadors,* hooded robes designed to hide the female form. The coach claimed that the extra clothing added ten seconds over a 500-meter course. Although Muslim peoples differ, in general those of Islamic faith have been little concerned about athletics and have contributed few champions to world sports.

There have been notable exceptions. Runner Hassiba Boulmerka became the first Algerian to win a world championship in 1991, and she was denounced by Muslim clerics at home for "running with naked legs in front of men." She, nonetheless, persisted in spite of death threats and took a gold medal in the 1,500-meter run at the 1992 Olympics. Another example is Hakeem Olajuwon, a Nigerian Muslim who is a star for the Houston Rockets professional basketball team. He rigidly fasts during Ramadan and even refuses water during games. In his case his average points per game rose three points in 1997 during the fasting period. "Religion is supposed to help you," he said. "It isn't supposed to take anything away. It enhances my game."

South of the Sahara Desert, beyond the reach of Islam in the rain forests and table

Iranian shooter Lida Fariman trains during the women's 10-meter Olympic air-rifle event in 1996. Fariman was the first Iranian woman to take part in the Olympics since 1979.

lands, African tribes participated in varied traditional sports. There were canoe races on the upper Congo River, oxen races in the mountains of Lesotho, and ball dances in southern Africa. Balls were made of wood or fresh hippopotamus hide, hammered until round and elastic. Both men and women performed dances in which they threw and caught the ball. The men would take turns, throw it high in the air, and then perform barking imitations of wild dogs before catching the falling ball. The women would form two lines and throw small balls made of roots under their legs to a person in the opposite line.

The sport most commonly found in Africa, however, was wrestling. It was a contest usually matching two adolescent boys who performed as a part of a puberty rite, or harvest celebration. In West Africa wrestling took place in the marketplace during the dry season when the boys could obtain a good foothold. The object was to throw the other person to the ground. At times there were intervillage competitions in which women fought other women, and sometimes women fought against men. Wrestling, moreover, sometimes became a part of marriage rituals, in which a man would have to dominate the woman, or fight other men in mock combat for the privilege of marrying a particular woman.

Wrestling also was a time-honored sport of the ancient Egyptian civilization (3100–332 B.C.) that flourished in the fertile Nile River Valley in northeast Africa. The rulers, known as pharoahs, along with the nobility demanded beauty and pleasure in life. They expressed a delight with the human form and had no inhibition about

nudity. Physical fitness was honored and the painted or carved figures of art reveal trim and fit people—only foreigners or stupid people were portrayed as fat. The royal official Ptahhotpe, in the middle of the third millennium (2300 B.C.), moreover, noted a distinction between the ideas of work and leisure. He wrote: "Do no more than you are ordered to, nor shorten the time accorded to leisure. It is hateful to the spirit to be robbed of the time for merriment." A tombstone from the 20th century B.C. carried an inscription, "I am one who used every day to the full, wasting no part of it. Never did I miss a moment of bliss." Accordingly, for the upper classes and the pharaoh at least, there was time for recreation and sport.

This attitude made possible the carvings and paintings of Egyptian life that are found on the tombs of the elite. This is the major source of information about Egyptian sports. In the tomb of Ptahhotpe at Saqqara in lower Egypt, for example, there are bas-relief carvings, in which the figures are carved so that they are slightly raised from the surrounding stone, that show naked boys wrestling and playing children's games. Others, dressed in short skirts, box with unprotected hands. A tomb painting at Beni Hasan on the Nile River 200 miles south of Alexandria shows 122 pairs of men and boys wrestling. This is the earliest depiction of wrestling grips, and the pictures indicate that there were no holds barred in Egyptian wrestling. The sport probably was used for military training, as well as for entertainment. Hunting scenes are also common, and apparently it was a royal duty to kill hippopotamuses and other

Egyptian tomb paintings, like this one depicting bird hunting, provide the major source of information about ancient Egyptian sports.

wild animals that threatened the kingdom. In 3100 B.C. a hippopotamus carried off and killed King Narmer, the founder of the first dynasty. After that the pharaohs thought it was sufficient to have servants hunt the dangerous beasts while they looked on from a safe distance.

The Nile River was central to Egyptian civilization, and thus boating and swimming were common. There was even a special goddess of swimming, Wadjet, who was worshipped during the period of the Old Kingdom (2686–2181 B.C.). There is no evidence of swimming competitions, but there are pictures of jousting boatmen. Following the tradition of physical fitness for leaders, Pharaoh Amenophis II (1438–1412 B.C.) challenged his soldiers to compete in archery,

running, and rowing contests. "Nor was there anyone who could bend a bow like him, and no one excelled him in running against others. His arms were so strong that he was never faint when he grasped the oar and rowed abaft his arrow-swift ship, the best of a crew of two hundred," read an inscription at Giza. Of course, it might be questioned if anyone would dare beat a pharaoh in any contest even if it could be done.

Demonstrations of physical skill were often a part of celebrations and festivals. There was stick fighting similar to modern fencing, ball games, and acrobatic dancing. A frieze at Medinet Habu, an archaeological site near Luxor, commemorating a victory of Ramses II around 1160 B.C., shows grandstands with excited fans, 10 pairs of wrestlers in an arena, and an umpire who says, "Take care, you are here before your lord, the pharaoh!" Egyptians are wrestling captives, and final victory over downed foreign blacks and Asians is shown by an Egyptian with his arms raised in victory. Herodotus, the wandering Greek historian, observed similar athletic contests in Egypt with prizes of cattle, cloaks, and animal skins.

The centralized government of the ancient Egyptians did not organize regular athletic contests nor build permanent sites for competition, but their culture celebrated the physical aspects of humanity. Sport played a prominent role. Indeed, the oldest historical evidence of organized sports comes from this civilization. Ancient Egypt, moreover, represents the greatest development of sporting traditions in Africa, a legacy that was passed on to the younger civilizations of the Mediterranean Sea at Crete and Greece.

On the island of Crete and smaller nearby islands in the eastern Mediterranean, several cultures merged to form Minoan civilization (3000–1000 B.C.). A strong fleet protected the islands so that there was no need to build protective walls around the cities. The civilization evolved in peace as its seafaring merchants carried on an extensive trade in the region, including Mesopotamia and Egypt. The people built great palaces and worshipped a mother goddess in festivals that featured acrobatic sports. Although details of the religion remain unknown, hints about the festivals and sports are preserved in the artwork of the culture.

Scenes of a decorated drinking goblet from 1500 B.C. show two adult boxers with metal helmets and gloves, and then on a lower portion, a victorious boxer with his downed opponent, legs in the air. From the same period there is a fresco, a painting on plaster, on the island of Thira that shows two children of the same size boxing with their right hands covered with a glove. There is also evidence of wrestling, but the most startling athletic portrayals are the pictures of bull jumping in the paintings at the palace of Knossos at Crete.

As a part of a religious festival that is still not understood today, men and women acrobats vaulted over the backs of captured wild bulls. Wearing boots and loin cloths, smiling performers grasped the bull by the horns, straight on, and as the bull reared its head, the acrobat landed hands first on the back of the animal, did a somersault, and recovered afoot at the rear of the beast. The stunt may have been executed by doing a somersault to the back of the bull and then another to the ground. The bull was not sacred and was later sacrificed. The frescoes indicate that the festivals were well attended by spectators and apparently served both religious and entertainment purposes. The bull games symbolized the supremacy of a goddess religion over an older belief in the primacy of the wild bull.

For this artistic civilization the greatest enemy turned out to be nature. A volcanic explosion around 1470 B.C. destroyed most of Thira, caused high waves, and littered the nearby islands with lava and ash. The catastrophe was preserved in the Greek legend of Atlantis, the story of a fabulous city destroyed and lost under the sea. Afterward Greek immigrants of the Mycenaean culture partially restored the palace of Knossos, but Minoan civilization nevertheless declined.

Chapter 2
Greek and Roman Athletics

Myron's Discus Thrower is executed in a realistic style that captures the moment of action forever.

T he Mycenaeans, who lived on the mainland of Greece, provided an athletic link to the culture of Crete and the Middle East. Minoan features such as a figure eight appeared in Mycenaean religious rituals, and Mycenaean art depicted pictures of hunting from chariots. It is not known whether they actually held races, but these Greek ancestors had the capability of chariot racing, as did the Egyptians and the peoples of Mesopotamia. The Mycenaean culture began to languish around 1200 B.C., however, and migrating peoples poured into the area. Greek civilization (800–200 B.C.) emerged from this background.

Sometime around 700 B.C., a blind poet named Homer, who lived in Ionia, a part of ancient Greece on the coast of the Aegean Sea in what is now Turkey, wrote two epics, the *Iliad* and the *Odyssey*. The *Iliad* recorded the exploits of a Mycenaean army led by Agamemnon against the city of Troy to recover the kidnapped wife of Menelaus, the king of Sparta. The *Odyssey* was the story of Odysseus, one of the soldiers, who took 10 years to find his way home after the defeat of the Trojans at Troy. Almost noth-

ing is known about Homer or about the accuracy of the texts. He probably mixed folklore with information about his own time. The epics, nonetheless, provide the earliest knowledge about Greek sports, and much of what Homer said has been supported by archaeologists and historians.

The last part of the *Iliad* reported sporting contests held in honor of Patroclus, who had been killed in battle. Achilles, who was his friend, called the leaders of the Greeks together on flat land near the sea and designated various competitions and prizes. First was a two-horse chariot race won by Diomedes, who was awarded a young woman prisoner and a Trojan cauldron, a large kettle. Epeius won a mule at the boxing match after bragging that he would tear his opponent into pieces and smash his bones. He almost did so and the other contestant, head lolling and spitting blood, was dragged from the ring. Odysseus finished first in running, after praying to the goddess Athena for help. "Hear me goddess," he said. "I need your valuable aid. Come down and speed my feet." She tripped the man in the lead so that he slipped head-first, mouth open, through a pile of fresh cow dung. Achilles awarded Odysseus a beautiful silver bowl.

Other contests were held in wrestling, discus, armed combat with sword and shield, javelin, and archery. The competition was based on the skills of warfare, and the prizes were the spoils of war—cauldrons, gold, ingots of iron, women, horses, mules, and oxen. Achilles awarded prizes to almost everyone and settled quarrels between the contestants and among the spectators. He was the organizer of the event and the referee. The contestants were mainly officers of equal rank and there was a sense of fair play. When the rules were violated, even by the gods, people protested. The emotional elements of sports—the desire to

win, pain, greed for prizes, arguments among the fans, admiration of excellence, compassion for losers—were portrayed. All of the athletic requirements of physical skill, competition, and rules, moreover, were present in this earliest clear example of sport.

Homer provided a further example of Greek sports in the *Odyssey,* when Odysseus, homeward bound, was entertained as a guest of honor by the Phaeacians, a Greek people who lived on islands in the Aegean Sea. After dinner the hosts offered athletic contests in boxing, wrestling, running, jumping, and discus throwing as entertainment. Laodamas and Euryalos, young Phaeacians, rudely challenged Odysseus to try their games. Angered by

Athena: the Goddess of Victory

In Greek mythology, Athena was the daughter of Zeus, who was the most powerful of the gods. She was born, fully grown and armed, leaping from the forehead of her father and was her father's favorite. He trusted her with his breastplate and thunderbolt. Grey-eyed Athena was a warrior goddess who continually intervened in the Trojan War, and she obviously favored Odysseus during the running race at the funeral of Patroclus. In the chariot race at the same celebration, she assured the victory of another favor-

ite, Diomedes, by destroying the first-place chariot by means of a broken shaft. The driver was flung from the vehicle, bruised his forehead, and lost the skin from his elbows, mouth, and nose. He was left speechless, with tears in his eyes. Athena was the goddess of swift, clear action that led to success. Nike, a winged symbol of Athena, carried the wreath of triumph to the victors.

Athena also was noted for her interest in agriculture and handicrafts, particularly spinning and weaving. She wove the

robe that Hera wore to capture the love of Zeus. She was said also to have created the olive tree, the branches and leaves of which were used to signify victory at Olympia. She was the patron goddess of Athens, and its citizens celebrated her birth with the Panathena festival. The most famous surviving building of Greek civilization, the Parthenon on the acropolis of Athens, was dedicated to her. Nearby the Athenians built the small, exquisite temple of Athena Nike to immortalize her role as the goddess of victory.

The artist Phidas sculpted a statue of Athena dressed as a warrior that stood inside the Parthenon and dwarfed all its surroundings, as this scale model of the interior attests. The winged Nike appears in her right hand to crown her with a wreath.

In Homer's epic The Odyssey, *Odysseus slays the suitors who tried to woo his wife, Penelope.*

their impertinence, Odysseus picked up the heaviest discus and, without taking off his cloak, spun, and let loose the stone. The Phaeacians ducked as the low-flung disk hummed through the air and threatened to take their heads off. It went much farther than the efforts of others, and Odysseus said, "Now reach me that mark, young men, and then I will make another throw, as great as this, I think, or one even better." That settled the difficulty.

After reaching home, however, Odysseus faced another contest. Since Odysseus had been absent for a decade, various suitors tried to force his loyal wife, Penelope, to take another husband. She agreed, but only if they could bend the bow of her absent husband, attach a string, and fire an arrow through "every socket hollow" of 12 iron axheads. None could string the bow. Odysseus, disguised as a poor vagabond, however, easily slipped the bowstring into place and plucked it. The sound was like "the voice of a swallow," and the color drained from the faces of the suitors. They knew what was coming. Odysseus shot through the targets and then proceeded to slaughter those who had invaded his house and tried to claim his wife.

This sort of athletic contest is a part of ancient folklore. An Egyptian story told, for example, of a pharaoh's son who traveled to the Middle East and found that the ruler of Naharin had set up a contest for the hand of his only daughter. She lived in a house with a window 37 meters above the ground; the man who could leap to the window could marry her. Other princes were trying when the Egyptian arrived. He first observed their fruitless efforts from a distance and joined the effort only after the princess looked encouragingly at him from the window. Leaping mightily he reached the ledge where the princess greeted him with kisses and hugs. The Egyptian married the princess and lived happily ever after.

In Greek folklore, furthermore, there is the story of Pelops and the origin of chariot racing. Pelops, for whom southern Greece, the Peloponnese, was named, sought to marry Hippodamia, who was the daughter of King Oenomaus. Prospective suitors were required to drive her away in a chariot, followed by the king with his swift horses. If caught, the young men would be speared by the king. On arriving at the palace, Pelops noticed the heads of 12 men already mounted on the gateway. Pelops, however, bribed Myrtilus, the royal charioteer, to replace the bronze axle pins of the king's chariot with pins made of beeswax. Myrtilus was promised a night with Hippodamia as a reward.

During the chase, the king's chariot fell apart and Oenomaus was killed. Pelops married the beautiful Hippodamia, but to avoid fulfilling his promise, he threw Myrtilus from a cliff into the sea. It was strength and cunning that the Greek gods admired, not integrity. The curse of the dying Myrtilus, however, supposedly brought misery to the descendants of Pelops. The Greeks erected a shrine to Pelops as the founder of chariot racing at the site of the Olympic games.

Rarely united as a nation, the Greeks lived apart in small, self-reliant cities that flourished in fertile valleys. The most famous of these city-states were Athens, admired for democratic government and

A Greek warrior mounts a chariot driven by a slave in this detail from a 520 B.C. grave. Chariots like these were also used in racing.

universal education, and Sparta, noted for its military training and discipline. Fiercely independent, the Greeks once joined together to fight off the invading Persians. In 490 B.C. the Athenians surprised and defeated the Persians at the Battle of Marathon. Here, the legend of Pheidippides was born. Although Herodotus said that a messenger was sent to Sparta, the story was first outlined 500 years later by Plutarch (46–120 A.D.), a Greek biographer. (With so distant a story, the truth is questionable.)

According to the tale, when the Persians landed near Athens, Pheidippides, a professional courier, was sent from Athens to Sparta to ask for help. The Spartans said they could not aid at the moment because of religious reasons, and Pheidippides ran back with the bad news. He then joined the soldiers at Marathon, participated in the successful battle, and ran back to Athens with the good news of victory. He entered the agora, the central plaza, of Athens, and announced the success: "Rejoice, we conquer!" Pheidippides then collapsed and died. Pheidippides, wearing full armor—shield, helmet, shin guards, sword—had run some 350 miles over hilly trails in five days' time. Although the literal truth of the story is doubtful, the idea of the modern marathon race came from this heroic legend.

The Persians, however, were not finished. They tried again to conquer Greece in 480 B.C., and 300 Spartans gave their lives to delay the Persians at Thermopylae. The Athenian navy thereafter destroyed the Persian fleet at Salamis, and in 479 B.C. the Greeks scattered the remainder of the invading army. The Persians gave up and the Greeks maintained their independence. The Greek city-states, however, even though they shared similarities in culture, could not coexist in peace. Pericles (495–429 B.C.), the leading statesman of Athens, aggressively led his city into a disastrous fight with its Spartan rivals. The Peloponnesian War (431–404 B.C.) resulted in the partial defeat and decline of Athens.

Nonetheless, the greatest development of sports before modern times occurred in ancient Greece. No Greek city was complete without a "gymnasium," a place set aside for exercise. There was space for outdoor games, bathing pools, wrestling facilities, and halls for massage. At the height of cultural development in Athens during the 5th century B.C., boys and men received instruction in wrestling, boxing, running, ball games, and general hygiene at the gymnasium. Successful athletes were honored as heroes of the city and served as coaches for the next generation. They are shown in art carrying long sticks to swat pupils who made mistakes.

Local festivals, such as the Panathenaea in Athens, featured musical competitions, chariot racing, trireme (large ships propelled by three banks of oars) races, torch relays, and male beauty contests. Women were excluded except from the processions. Athenians devoted their leisure time to sport and celebrated athletics with painted vases, poetry, coins, and statues. The vases of Athenian potters covered with athletic scenes now serve as a chief source of information about Greek sports.

Obvious was not only a love of sports, but also a celebration of the human body. As with the Egyptians and Minoans, there was little hesitation about nudity, especially male nudity, and Greek art attempted to portray a perfect, well-proportioned figure. The concept of *arete,* excellence in all aspects of life, applied. Furthermore, there was to be harmony, or balance. According to Plato (427–348 B.C.), one of the great Athenian philosophers and a wrestler, a person should educate both body and mind. The Greeks applied these ideals to athletics, at least at first.

The most important events in Greek sports history were the four Panhellenic, or all-Greek, "crown" games. Delphi, Corinth, Nemea, and Olympia hosted athletic celebrations for the gods, where the awards were wreaths, or leafy crowns. They started as local celebrations that grew and attracted other Greeks. The crown games were scheduled so that at least one of them occurred every year. The earliest, and the one that has modern significance, was the festival at Olympia, an old religious site sacred to Artemis, the goddess of the hunt, and Zeus, the most powerful of gods, in the hills of the western Peloponnese.

It might be argued that women were the first to use the place for a footrace of virgins. Legend stated that Hippodamia, out of gratitude for marriage to Pelops, gathered 16 women for the first *Heraia*, a festival in honor of Hera, the wife of Zeus. Every four years, local women organized this event, which featured 16 virgins. They were divided into three age categories; wore a chiton, or tunic, that reached a little above the knee and bared the right breast; ran footraces; and were given olive wreaths as awards. The Temple of Hera was the first structure at the Olympic site, and in later years after the Olympics fully evolved, the women used the stadium track, which was shortened by one-sixth for their races.

The Olympics, however, developed primarily as a celebration for male athletes. The first meeting in 776 B.C. recorded a winner, Coroebus of Elis, who sprinted the length of a "stade," about 200 yards, or the length of the stadium. The first meeting was a one-day, local celebration, but in 724 B.C. the officials added a two-length race. In 720 B.C. they included an endurance run of 20 to 24 lengths; in 708 B.C., a pentathlon of running, jumping, discus, javelin, and wrestling; in 688 B.C., boxing; in 680 B.C., four-horse chariot racing; and in 648 B.C., horseback riding and the pankration, which was a combination of boxing and wrestling.

After this there were modifications, but many athletic skills were represented. Curiously, the events did not include archery, ball games, or swimming, although these other sports were known to the Greeks. The Olympic games, nonetheless, evolved into five days of competition with official sacrifices to the gods. They continued every four years for more than 1,100 years, until the Christian emperor Theodosius of Rome halted the contests in 393 A.D. because he thought they were non-Christian.

Vases like this one, filled with oil from the olive trees sacred to the goddess Athena, were awarded to winners in the athletic contests at the Panathenaea. At this major Athenian festival, the footrace was the prized event.

For much of the time the event was organized and controlled by the Eleans, who ruled the province where Olympia was located. Every four years heralds wearing olive wreaths went to the Greek city-states to announce the date of the games and proclaim the Olympic truce. This was a time of peace, at first one month and then later three months, that allowed contestants and fans to travel safely to and from the celebration. In this span there was to be no warfare, no robbery, no legal disputes, and no executions of criminals. Competitors were expected to come to the site one month early to practice under the supervision of the Olympic officials. An athlete was also required to be a free-born Greek citizen, with no criminal record, and trained in his sport for at least 10 months.

When they arrived at Olympia, the athletes found various places for athletic competition, temples, and training facilities. These were built over time. The earliest was the Temple of Hera, which was constructed with wooden pillars around 600 B.C. The pillars were replaced with lime-stone columns as the wood rotted. The altar ruins of this temple serve today as the traditional spot for the lighting of the Olympic torch, which is then sent in relays to the site of the modern games.

The most important religious site, however, was the Temple of Zeus, which was completed in 456 B.C. It had 34 columns, a marble tile roof, and drain spouts in the form of lions' heads. Inside there was a hollow, seated statue of Zeus, 13 meters high, made of gold and ivory. In his left hand he held a scepter and in the palm of his right hand he held Nike, the winged messenger of victory. His throne, studded with gold, ivory, ebony, and precious stones, was painted and carved with figures. The statue, considered one of the "seven wonders of the ancient world," was destroyed by fire in the 4th century A.D.

There were other smaller temples, lodging facilities, training areas, and a bathing pool built in the 5th century B.C. Water supply was a problem at the site, one that was solved only after a Roman millionaire, Herodes Atticus, constructed a fountain

This reconstruction shows Olympia as it looked at the time of the first Olympic games. Archaeological excavations of the city revealed several temples as well as the stadium.

system in the 2nd century A.D. The important athletic facilities included the stadium, which was 192.27 meters long. According to legend, it was measured by the famous Hercules, who placed one foot in front of the other 600 times. An alternative story said that it was the distance he could run without taking a breath. Be that as it may, all Greek stadiums were approximately, but not exactly, this length. It was a measurement known as a "stade," from which the word *stadium* derives. In practicality, it was a distance that a man could run at an all-out sprint.

The clay and sand track down the center had stone starting blocks embedded at each end. Cut with two grooves, the blocks provided a grasp for bare feet and a standing start. The only seats were on a judges' platform; the spectators were expected to lounge on the surrounding grass embankments. The stadium had a trough to carry drinking water, and could accommodate about 45,000 people. It also had a 32-meter-long tunnel, probably built later by Romans, that served as a grand entrance for the athletes.

The facilities at Olympia also included a hippodrome, or place to race horses and chariots. The word *hippodrome* comes from the Greek language, *hippos* meaning horse, and *dromos* meaning race course. It was an oval approximately 200 meters wide and 600 meters long, with two posts to mark the turns. There was a judges' stand, seating for spectators on the surrounding embankments, and probably a wall to protect the fans from out-of-control horses and chariots. The site was later washed away by floods, but an observer in the 2nd century

A.D. noted the use of a special starting gate that allowed chariots and horses to begin their races on an even line.

Knowledge about the site comes from German archaeologists who began excavations in 1875. The land was covered with four meters of silt at that time. The second major source of information is the preserved comments of Pausanias, a tourist from Lydia (now in Turkey) who visited Olympia in 174 A.D. Not much is known about him, but he was curious, uncritical, and honest. He recorded much of what he saw in detail, and told, for example, about the starting gate of the hippodrome:

The starting place is shaped like the prow of a ship . . . at the very tip of the beak is a bronze dolphin on a rod. Each side of the starting place is more than four hundred feet long, and in each of the sides, stalls are built. . . . In front of the chariots or race-horses stretches a rope as a barrier. . . . On the altar is a bronze eagle, with its wings spread to the full. The starter sets the machinery in the altar going, whereupon up jumps the eagle into the view of the spectators, and down falls the dolphin to the ground. The first ropes to be let go are those at the furthest ends of the prow, and the horses stationed here are the first off. Away they go until they come neck and neck with the chariots that have drawn the second stations. Then the ropes at the second stations are released. And so it runs on till all the chariots are abreast of each other at the beak of the prow. After that it is for the charioteers to display their skill and the horses their speed.

Pausanias wandered the grounds and read the inscriptions on the statues of great athletes and on the "zanes," which were

bronze images of Zeus paid for by fines on those who had cheated. Two boxers, for example, who secretly agreed on the outcome of their match in advance, contributed to the zanes. Pausanias also noted the story about an enemy of the famous athlete Theagenes who had won 1,400 times in various contests. His foe came every night to whip the statue of the dead athlete. This ended when the statue fell and killed the abuser. Then the dead man's relatives prosecuted the sculpture for murder and the statue of Theagenes was dropped into the sea. Famine followed, however, and upon the advice of the priestess at Delphi the statue was fished out and restored to its proper place.

Pausanias also provided information about women at the Olympic games. They were not only banned from direct participation in the games, but also prevented from watching. The law was that guilty women would be cast off a nearby cliff. Pausanias, however, wrote that the only one ever caught was forgiven. She was a widow whose son was competing in 404 B.C., and she came disguised as a trainer. Upon his victory, Callipateira, the widow, leaped over an enclosure to congratulate him and exposed her sex. The officials forgave her, however, because her father, brothers, and son were all champions. After that, however, the Eleans required all coaches to strip before entering the arena.

The role of women at Olympia is still unclear, however. Pausanias noted that the priestess of Demeter, goddess of fertility, had a special seat at the stadium. Before the Olympics began, the area was sacred for Demeter. Also, apparently there was no rule prohibiting virgins, only married women. Furthermore, women who owned horses could win at Olympia even though they could not drive or watch them perform. The victory award went to the owner of the horses, not to the rider or driver. A fragment of black marble found at Olympia dating from 396 B.C. stated, "Kyneska, victorious at the chariot race with her swift-footed horses, erected this statue. I assert that I am the only woman in all Greece who won this crown." The exact role of women at the Olympic games remains a puzzle.

The contestants at Olympia were men, who competed naked. Supposedly, in 720 B.C. a sprinter, Orsippos, lost his loincloth while running and discovered that a nude man could run faster than others. After that, the other athletes, led by the Spartans, shed their clothes. They ran one- and two-length sprints, a distance race of 20 to 24 lengths, and in 520 B.C. added a two-stade race in armor. The men wore greaves, or shin guards, and a helmet. They also carried a heavy round shield. The race, which was filled with the mishaps of dropped equipment, must have made a clanking, clattering noise. Although the race had obvious overtones of war, it may also have provided comic entertainment before the final day of feasting and awarding of olive wreaths to all the Olympic victors.

Combat duels of wrestling, boxing, and pankration apparently took place in the palaistra, a partially enclosed training area. For wrestling there was a rule to prohibit gouging in the genitals, mouth, eyes, or other tender parts of the body. The athletes anointed themselves with olive oil and then dusted with powder before the competi-

tion. In upright wrestling, now called Greco-Roman style, three falls meant a loss. In ground wrestling victory came only after one man admitted defeat by raising the index finger of the right hand. In boxing as in wrestling, there were no weight limits and the fight continued without breaks until a victor was determined. On occasion, evenly matched boxers agreed to exchange undefended blows in order to decide a winner. In general, fighters aimed at the head and protected their hands with leather thongs. The match ended when one man gave up or was knocked out.

For the pankration, a combination of wrestling and boxing, the object was also to gain submission. Although gouging, kicking, and biting were forbidden, the sport was unusually rough. For example, Sostratos from Sikyon, who caught the notice of Pausanias, became famous as "Mr. Finger-Tips" for his technique of breaking fingers. "Mr. Jumping Weight," a Cilician (from what is now the Armenian part of Turkey), was famous for his trick of throwing his opponents to the ground, holding onto a foot, and twisting the leg out of its socket. Pausanias also noticed at Phigaleia a statue dedicated to Arrhachion, who died in a pankration bout in 564 B.C. In the fight his opponent squeezed Arrachion's middle with his legs and strangled him, hands on his throat, at the same time. As he expired Arrachion dislocated his competitor's toe and made him surrender. Arrachion then died, and the judges crowned his corpse with the olive wreath.

In the stadium the men hurled discuses of bronze, apparently, with feet planted and using only a three-quarters turn for mo-

Milo: Death by Conceit

In the middle of the 6th century B.C., Milo of Croton won six wrestling victories at Olympia, one of these in the boys' division. On the seventh attempt he was beaten by a younger man who merely refused to grapple with him and stayed out of reach until Milo collapsed from exhaustion. Even with that, the new champion and cheering fans picked Milo up to parade him around the stadium on their shoulders. He was popular and many tales were told about him.

Supposedly, Milo once carried an entire cooked bull around the stadium before he sat down to eat the whole carcass. A critic said that the bull when alive moved his body with less exertion than Milo and that the bull's mind was not worth anything, "just about like Milo's." The wrestler also was said to have once drunk nine liters of wine at one sitting in order to win a bet. He demonstrated his strength by tying a cord around his forehead. By holding his breath, so it was said, he could swell the veins in his head and break the cord. He once won victory with a "bye," an automatic advance through an event, because no one would wrestle with him. On the way to receive his olive wreath, he slipped and the crowd jeered that he should not be crowned because he fell. Milo growled, "That is not three falls. I fell only once; let someone give me the other two falls."

Pausanias, the tourist who commented about Olympia, recorded the story of his death. While traveling the countryside, Milo came upon a fallen, drying tree trunk into which a farmer had driven wedges. With excessive pride in his strength, the wrestler thought to complete the splitting of the log by pulling it apart with his hands. As he did so the wedges fell out and the log snapped back on his fingers. He was trapped, and that night Milo was eaten by wolves. His story confirmed Homer's warning in *The Iliad* that those who glory in their strength perish by it.

mentum. Javelins were launched after a short run. The athletes tied a thong around the middle of the shaft, looped it around their fingers, and let it unravel as they hurled the javelin toward a target. The thong gave a spiral to the spear and made it easier to guide. This might have been important because, like the discus, the javelin event was held where spectators might be injured by an inaccurate throw. The long jump, also a stadium event, provided a mystery because no one today knows how it was accomplished. The Greeks carried weights, called *halteres,* in each hand, and leaped from a standing start. They probably used a series of rhythmic hops, because a record of 16.66 meters was recorded in the middle of the 5th century B.C. The ancient Greek record may be questionable, but for comparison, the current triple jump record is 17.77 meters.

Horse racing and chariot events were conducted in the hippodrome. Both two-horse and four-horse chariot contests were difficult and dangerous because the teams made complete circular loops around the end posts and raced as far as eight miles. There was no median strip in the Greek hippodromes to prevent head-on colli-sions. Pindar (518–438 B.C.), a poet who often wrote of athletic victories, noted that at Delphi all but one of 40 chariots crashed in a single race. Accidents were so frequent and dangerous that chariot owners hired drivers. The owners, however, were the ones crowned champion. The same situation was true for the horse races, and the jockeys who rode bareback were usually paid servants.

The pentathlon called for an athlete of many skills. In one afternoon the men competed in five events—discus throwing, jumping, javelin throwing, running, and wrestling. It is unknown how victory was counted, but it may be that after winning three events a person could claim first place and the competition stopped. Although the pentathletes were not as popular as other athletes, seemingly their overall training gave them a supple body admired by such critics as Aristotle (384–322 B.C.), the Greek philosopher. "Each age has its own beauty," he said. "In youth, it lies in the possession of a body capable of enduring all kinds of contests. . . . It is for this reason that pentathletes are the most beautiful; they are naturally adapted both for exertion of the body and swiftness of foot." Overdevel-

The Pentathlon, consisting of discus, running, jumping, javelin, and wrestling events was the measure of an all-around athlete.

oped muscles, demanded by the combat sports, violated the Greek ideal of beauty. This ideal suffered as time passed. During the 8th century B.C., most of the contestants in the Olympic games came from the Peloponnese, the lower part of Greece. Spartans, who sought overall fitness for war, dominated the events at that time and through the 7th century B.C. They influenced the inclusion of combative events. At the beginning of the 7th century B.C., however, champions from Athens and Thebes were recorded, and in 688 B.C. the winning boxer came from Smyrna, a seaport in what is now Turkey. The games had become popular. More athletes competed, they specialized in specific events, and Spartan victories became rare.

Because athletes were well rewarded, professionalism became quite common in the 5th and 4th centuries B.C. Athens, for example, gave free meals and pots of valuable olive oil to its heroes. Although the athletes won only olive leaves at Olympia, they could make money by entering local games, of which there were several hundred. In 420 B.C. the Athenian playwright Euripides wrote:

Of the thousands of evils which exist in Greece there is no greater evil than the race of athletes. In the first place, they are incapable of living, or of learning to live, properly. Brute strength and win-

ning ultimately became the goal of Greek athletics. The older ideal of balance in mind and body was lost.

Still, for the spectator the Olympic games held enormous appeal. While commenting on the need to endure discomfort in the quest for knowledge, Epictetus (50–130 A.D.), the Roman stoic philosopher, said:

There are unpleasant and difficult things in life. But don't they happen at Olympia? Don't you suffer from the heat? Aren't you cramped for space? Don't you bathe badly? Don't you get soaked whenever it rains? Don't you get your fill of noise and shouting and other annoyances? But I suspect that you compare all this to the value of the show and endure it.

Another commentator, Lucian (120–180 A.D.), a Greek satirist and Roman official, wrote:

If the Olympic Games were being held now . . . you would be able to see for yourself why we attach such great importance to athletics. No one can describe in mere words the extraordinary . . . pleasure derived from them and which you yourself would enjoy if you were seated among the spectators feasting your eyes on the prowess and stamina of the athletes, the beauty and power of their bodies, their incredible dexterity and skill, their invincible strength, their courage, ambition, endurance and tenacity. You would never stop . . . applauding them.

In the course of the first 800 years B.C., the Greeks colonized the southern part of the Italian Peninsula while a mysterious group of people, the Etruscans, settled in the center and north. Information about them comes mainly from burial chambers

The original statue of Zeus at Olympia was one of the Seven Wonders of the Ancient World. It was destroyed in the 5th century, but other representations of the god survive, such as this statue of Phidias cradling the head of Zeus.

dating from the 6th century B.C. Paintings on the walls show people running, dancing, wrestling, boxing, throwing the discus, jumping, and swimming. Both men and women athletes are shown; a small statue from the 4th century B.C. shows a man wrestling with a woman. Unusual, and disturbing, however, are the bloody scenes showing armed combat between prisoners and fights between men and beasts. At the Tomb of Augurs at Tarquinia, a blindfolded man is shown fighting a dog with a club. Another man controls the contest with ropes tied to the wrist of the man and to the collar of the dog. This bloodthirsty taste seems indeed to have been inherited by the Romans.

Etruscans built the town of Rome in the 8th century B.C. as their capital and ruled until they were pushed out by Latin tribespeople at the end of the 6th century B.C. Latins, or Romans, then spread by conquest through the Italian Peninsula and beyond. By the middle of the 2nd century B.C., Rome had taken Greece and by the end of the 1st century B.C. it controlled most of the countries around the Mediterranean Sea. This empire was sustained until the end of the 5th century A.D. by well-trained and -disciplined armies. If officers judged a unit cowardly, they called out every tenth man and required the other soldiers to beat them to death. Understandably, soldiers feared their officers more than their enemies.

At the time of the first emperor, Augustus (31 B.C.–14 A.D.), Rome began two centuries of peace, the *pax romana,* during which most of the fighting took place on distant frontiers. To maintain their warrior tradi-

tion, the Romans moved the fighting to artificial battlefields in the stadiums of cities. Their sports reflect their interest in combat, with an easy tolerance for cruelty and death. Soldiers were trained in running, jumping, swimming, spear throwing, archery, and wrestling. Following the Greek example, the governors of cities built public baths where people could play ball games, converse, and rest. Balls, made of leather and either stuffed with hair or filled with air, were used to play noisy contests of keep-away. Like the Greeks, the Romans exercised first and bathed afterward.

Roman governors were expected to build stadiums for spectator sports. In Rome, particularly after the time of Augustus, emperors needed to provide spectacles for the entertainment of a restless, bored, and largely unemployed populace. The number of official holidays grew from 88 per year in the 1st century to 176 in the 4th century. Games for the holidays, along with free bread for the spectators, were organized by state officials. There were also special festivities, such as the celebration of Emperor Trajan's victory over the Dacians in 108–9 A.D., which lasted for 123 days. On this occasion 9,138 gladiators fought and 11,000 animals died.

At its height Rome had five amphitheaters and two large stadiums for public use. The most famous stadium was the Circus Maximus, 600 by 200 meters with a sand track, originally built by the Etruscans in the center of town. The Romans expanded it to hold about 200,000 people in three tiers and used it largely for chariot races. Chariots had lost their wartime usefulness, but were symbolic in Roman religion. Jupiter,

the most powerful god, was portrayed riding in a chariot. The races, which were dedicated to Jupiter, therefore, had religious significance. Teams designated by colors—white, red, green, and blue—attracted fan loyalty, organized cheering, and gambling. The charioteers were professionals who received gifts and became celebrities. Rivalry between stables led to bribery, attempts to hire the best drivers, and efforts to poison opposing horses.

The races involved two-horse, four-horse, six-horse, or ten-horse teams circling the course seven times. There would be from 10 to 24 races per day, usually involving four teams per race. The 180-degree turns at the posts were points of collisions where often a race ended in a bloody, dirty pile of injured horses and humans, harnesses, and splintered chariots. The drivers, who wound the reins around their bodies while racing, carried sharp knives to cut themselves loose. Otherwise, frightened horses emerging from a crash would drag the charioteer to death. So popular was this sport that it outlasted the Roman Empire by 500 years. Historian Ammianus Marcellinus from Antioch commented in the early 4th century A.D.:

Now let me describe for you this mass of people, unemployed and therefore with too much time on their hands. For them the Circus Maximus is temple, home, social club and center

The Roman Colosseum was one of the important stadiums of the ancient world. The ruins are now a major tourist attraction in Rome.

of all their hopes. You can see them beyond the city, arguing about the races . . . and declaring that the country will come to ruin unless their favorite wins in the next races. And on the day they all rush to the circus even before daybreak, to secure a place.

The most famous Roman amphitheater was the Colosseum, which was completed in 82 A.D. with a capacity for 50,000 people. It had three tiers of seats, 80 entrances, awnings for shade, fountains for cool air, and a wooden arena floor 200 feet by 280 feet. There was a 15-foot-high wall topped by an iron grate to separate the spectators from the floor. Beneath the floor were cages for captive animals and humans. Here, the shocking blood sports of Rome took place that pitted humans against humans, animals against animals, and humans against animals. The Romans delighted in watching elephants fight tigers or crocodiles. Men called *bestiarii* were trained to kill lions and other wild animals with spears. The human competitions usually involved gladiators.

The first recorded fight between gladiators took place in 264 B.C. It was a presentation by two aristocrats in honor of their dead father, and only three pairs of fighters took part. In 65 B.C. Julius Caesar (100–44 B.C.), who owned his own gladiator training school, gave funeral games for his father that involved 640 fighters clad in silver armor. Emperor Augustus tried to fix the upper limit at 120 gladiators per show, but this was largely ignored by the politicians, who tried to outdo one another. In the 1st century the state took control of the sport, and by the end of the century the gladiator schools could supply 10,000 combatants at any time.

The recruits of the schools came from the Roman lower classes, criminals, slaves, or from foreign captives. They fought with their native weapons, swords and shields and daggers, but also learned the art of ensnaring an opponent with a net and stabbing with a trident, a spear with a three-pronged point. The schools provided trainers, doctors, and others needed for the sport. At a festival the gladiators first formed a procession and addressed the emperor with the words, *Morituri te salutant* (Those who are about to die salute you). During the fight the spectators would yell and scream "Kill!" or "Strike!" The fight sometimes ended in the death of one of the gladiators, and a wounded man might ask for mercy by laying aside his arms and raising his index finger. The raucous crowd voted thumbs up for life, or thumbs down for death, but the final decision was the emperor's. The gladiator might be spared if he had given a good fight. Also, because gladiators were "rented" for the occasion, a "thumbs down" meant that the school had to be paid for a dead gladiator. Therefore, most combats did not end in death.

Dead men in the Colosseum were hauled out by slaves dressed in costumes of the underworld. One dressed as Hermes, the Greek god who conducted the dead to the underworld, tested the body with a red-hot iron to be certain the gladiator was not faking in order to escape. A second slave dressed as Charon, the Etruscan god of

death, with long boots and a bird mask, tapped the body with a mallet to symbolize death taking possession of the dead. The attendants sprinkled sand over pools of blood, smoothed the floor, and made way for more combatants. Contests between armed women and between midgets were later added to the games.

The Colosseum, which gave spectators an intimate view, was also the site for executions and gory enactments of plays. As the story of Orpheus was recited, for example, a wild boar was released onto the floor to tear the actor to pieces. The usual course of events, however, featured animal fights in the morning, criminal executions by half-starved beasts at noon, and gladiator combat in the afternoon. Seneca (4 B.C.–65 A.D.), a Roman philosopher and politician, commented about his visit to the Colosseum: "I came home more greedy, more cruel and inhuman. Man, a sacred thing to man, is killed for sport and merriment."

The Roman blood lust was not tempered by contact with Greek sports, but the Romans were impressed with the pankration and with boxing. The Romans added metal spikes to the boxer's thongs to make the contest a bloody, life-and-death matter. In 186 B.C. Greek athletes gave a demonstration in Rome, but the prudish Romans were shocked by Greek nudity. Romans, nevertheless, spread the Olympic games through the empire and restored the facilities at Olympia. In 67 A.D. Emperor Nero

(37–68 A.D.) forced a special scheduling of the games and drove a chariot with a 10-horse team. During the race, he fell out of the chariot and failed to complete the course. He nonetheless was crowned with an olive wreath. In gratitude he granted freedom to the whole province and gave cash rewards to the judges. After Nero committed suicide the next year his name was erased from the list of champions and the cash was returned.

In 395 A.D., however, the Roman Empire divided into two segments. The western part, with its capital at Rome, disintegrated under the pressure of barbarian invasions in 410, 455, and 476. The stadium contests disappeared with it. There was also pressure from the Roman Catholic Church, which viewed sports as pagan. For that reason Emperor Theodosius I (347–95), the last ruler of a united Roman Empire, officially decreed the end of the Olympic games in 393. Greek temples and sporting facilities were thereafter destroyed. The Colosseum and the Circus Maximus, where the chariot races were held, fell into ruins.

The eastern portion of the Roman Empire, with its capital at Constantinople, developed into the Byzantine Empire, which endured until 1453. Gladiator contests in the eastern part ended shortly after the division, however, and fights with animals lasted only until the end of the 5th century. There was Christian opposition to these sports throughout the old empire. Supported by the emperor, chariot racing, however, continued at the hippodrome of Constantinople, a venue that could seat 60,000 people. A variation was introduced. A loser in the morning could challenge the winner for an afternoon race with horses and chariot exchanged in order to test the skill of the driver. Byzantium embraced other sports—archery, fencing with sticks, running—and imported from Persia in the first half of the 5th century a game that was like lacrosse played on horseback. It was enjoyed by the nobility, those who could afford sports horses.

The time of great spectator sports was over until the modern era. The Romans, however, demonstrated the use of large stadiums and the appeal of athletic competition for major segments of a population. They also left a legacy of blood lust, an element that still lingers in some sports today.

Roman mobs inside the Colosseum turn thumbs down and yell "Occide!" ("Kill!") as a fallen gladiator raises his hand for mercy. Some of the Colosseum's old cellars, where gladiators waited their turn in the bloody games, have been restored and opened to the public.

CALEDONIANS.

COME a' THEGITHER.

AND GET THE NEXT

SCOTTISH-AMERICAN

JOURNAL

WHICH WILL CONTAIN A FULL REPORT OF THE

CALEDONIAN GAMES

ORDER IT FROM NEWSDEALERS.

SCOTTISH-AMERICAN PRINT, No. 33 Rose Street, New York.

Chapter 3

The Sports of Early Western Civilization

I n the thousand years after the fall of Rome, Asian and Islamic civilizations directed the course of history. Much of southern and western Europe retreated before the onslaught of Viking and Saracen raiders along the coastlines. People living on the land took refuge when necessary in neighboring castles. In the later part of the Middle Ages (500–1500) this feudal system gave way to the formation of nations such as England and France. This developing Western civilization inherited some ideals and sports from the bygone Greeks and Romans. The peasants and nobility of Europe, meanwhile, added their own traditional sports.

The peasants played various ball games. A type of field hockey, called "hurling" by the Irish and "shinty" by the Scots, was popular among the Celtic peoples. The Germans and Dutch enjoyed "kegels," or "kegeln," which was a bowling game that used wooden balls to knock over upright blocks, or cones, of wood. This evolved into a Dutch nine-pin game called "skittles." An English and French version required the bowler to roll a ball into a target zone. Curling, developed in Scotland on frozen lakes, was bowling on ice with "curling stones" equipped with handles. The idea was to glide the stone into a target area, with the stones closest to the center gaining the most points. Immigrants took the sport to Canada, and *The Encyclopedia of North American Sports History* by Ralph Hickock quotes a French-Canadian farmer near Quebec from 1835: "Today I saw a band of Scotchmen who were throwing large balls of iron like tea-kettles on the ice, after which they cried 'Soop! Soop!' and then laughed like fools. I really believe they *are* fools." An outsider who witnesses modern curling with team members busily sweeping the ice to influence the direction of the sliding stone might well agree.

At Derby in England, entire villages challenged other villages to play a type of football in which people tried to kick, carry, or throw a ball toward an opponent's goal. The goal was a waterwheel in one case, a gate in another. Inspired by ale on Fat Tuesday, the day before the holy season of Lent, the villagers bit, hit, and mauled one another. There were few rules. People used the ball game to settle old grievances, and the result was bruises, broken limbs, and

This 1885 issue of Caledonians, *a Scottish-American journal, depicts (from left) a caber toss, bagpiping, the Highland Fling dance, stone throwing, and hammer throwing.*

Curling is a major winter sport of Scotland and is governed internationally by the Royal Caledonia Curling Club. This curling match pits Scotland against America.

sometimes death. Although English monarchs tried to suppress the celebration because of the injuries—better that the peasants practice something practical, like archery—this forerunner of modern rugby nonetheless continued.

The Scots also held village competitions that required throwing stones and sledgehammers for distance, weights and bundles of hay for height, and long poles (cabers) end-over-end for accuracy. The caber toss could also be found in Italy, France, Germany, and Sweden. In colonial America the caber toss was known as "ye casting of ye bar." Dances, such as the Highland Fling, bagpipe playing, and running became a part of the Scottish town festivities. In modern times Scottish immigrants have revived these traditional activities, and they have become a particularly popular ethnic celebration in the United States, Canada, and Europe.

English milkmaids, meanwhile, devised one of the earliest bat and ball games. One woman threw a ball to knock over a three-legged milking stool. The other made points by successfully defending the stool with a broom, but was out if the pitcher caught a fly ball. When that happened the women

exchanged positions. Stoolball was thus the forerunner of the modern games of cricket and baseball. In the stables of the rich at the same time, the peasant groomsmen played quoits. Two horseshoes were bound together to form a circle and thrown at a peg. The one who came closest or ringed the peg won the match. The modern game of horseshoes invented by American frontiersmen came from this game of pitching at a target.

Informal horse racing, hunting, and falconry (hunting birds with the use of falcons, or other birds of prey) were sports of the upper classes. The most spectacular activity of the elite, however, was the tourney. Derived from warfare between armored knights, it was used to keep fighting skills sharp. The mock battles of the tournament, however, were conducted with dull weapons. Although the purpose was not to hurt the warriors, injury was difficult to avoid when they wore 125-pound suits of armor and fell seven feet from the backs of war horses when knocked off. The melee was common in the early tournaments, and the joust in later ones. The melee involved a general free-for-all fight in a large, open area with large numbers of knights banging away on each other with swords and maces. The object was to remain in the saddle after others had fallen. In 1249 near Cologne a melee left 60 unhorsed, trampled knights dead or dying from wounds and suffocating in the dust.

A joust was a duel between two knights who galloped on horseback down either side of a barrier and tried to hit the other with the tip of a lance. A strike on the breastplate was worth a point; on the head was two points; unhorsed was a clear loss. Knights left their helmets unbolted so that if hit in the head the helmet would slip off. Otherwise, they might be not only unhorsed, but decapitated as well. Tournaments were held with great pageantry and attended by the nobility of the region. However, the practice of this kind of sport-warfare lost its importance after the invention of the longbow and firearms. These weapons could penetrate the armor and made the knight obsolete. The tourney faded away in the 16th century after Henry II of France (1519–59) died of an accidental head wound from a joust. The tip of his opponent's lance went through his visor and into an eye socket.

During the Renaissance period (1400–1700) of Western civilization, sword fighting gave rise to the sport of fencing. Baldesar Castiglione (1478–1529), an Italian aristocrat, advised gentlemen in his *Book of the Courtier,* which was published in 1528:

> Here, I believe, his first duty is to know how to handle expertly every kind of weapon. . . . For apart from their use in war, when perhaps the finer points may be neglected, often differences arise between one gentleman and another and lead to duels, and very often the weapons used are those that come immediately to hand. So, for safety's sake, it is important to know about them.

Sword fighting was the preferred means of self-defense for upper-class gentlemen in Italy and France, and they relied on experts to teach them. Italian fencing masters emphasized speed, skill, and the technique of lunging with the point. The French masters taught the use of balance and a thrust-parry-

riposte style of fighting. Thrust-parry-riposte meant that one fencer attacks with a thrust, the defender turns aside the thrust with a parry, and then counterattacks with a riposte. The fencers thus took turns attacking and defending. For practice the French invented the face mask for protection. Eventually three main forms of practice weapons—foil, épée, and sabre—evolved with their own techniques and scoring methods. Foil and épée are thrust weapons and points are scored only by touching with the tip. The sabre developed from cutting and slashing swords, and thus points can be made by using the edge of the blade as well as the point. From a means of self-defense, fencing subsequently evolved into a sport. Fencing remained popular with the upper classes in Europe, came later to the United

Tournaments, or mock battles, became both a way of keeping up fighting skills and of entertaining nobility in the Middle Ages. Though there was some variation, a typical lance was about 12 feet long and weighed about 10 pounds.

States, and was included among the events of the first modern Olympics in 1896.

Castiglione also recommended tennis to the upper class to demonstrate physical fitness. It was originally a type of handball played by French monks in monastery courtyards. They batted a ball made of leather and stuffed with hair over a rope strung across the yard. The object was to place the ball so that the opponent could not make a return shot, and to do so the monks used ricochet shots off walls and roof. At first players used bare hands for hitting the ball, then gloves, then webbing between the fingers, and finally in the 15th century a racket strung with strips of sheep intestines. This was the start of racket and paddle sports. The game spread, and by the 16th century Henry VIII of England (1491–1547) boasted seven rackets and a tennis court at Hampton Court, one of the oldest that is still in use.

The words concerning tennis are difficult to track, but according to Jean Jules Jusserand, a French diplomat and Pulitzer Prize–winning writer of the early 20th century, the name for tennis came from the French word *tenez*. Supposedly, this came from *tenetz,* meaning "take heed," which in this instance meant "get ready to play." The French also used the word *l'oeuf,* meaning "egg" or "zero." Some historians believe the English translated that into "love" for zero as part of the scoring of the game.

In England Charles II (1630–85), known as the "Merry Monarch," encouraged sports through his love of play and gambling. In 1681, for example, Charles selected a team of 12 men and challenged the Duke of Albemarle to do the same. The teams then competed in wrestling, fencing, and football. The king's team lost every contest, but he did not mind. His happiness was in gambling. Charles also was interested in bowling, sailing, and horse racing. He built a private racecourse, imported horses, and sometimes rode in the races himself.

Because gamblers wanted to keep horse races fair, they began to adopt standard rules. As early as 1722, some 112 English towns regularly held races. Around 1750 rich aristocrats formed the Jockey Club of London to set rules of proper dress for jockeys, appoint officials, and conduct fair races. Tattersalls, a market for buying and selling race horses, opened in 1766. Richard Tattersall (1724–95) founded a firm of horse auctioneers and gave his name to a popular textile design of colored lines that formed squares. The design was originally used for horse blankets. James Weatherby began publishing the *Racing Calendar* in

Court tennis as practiced in the 16th century differs from the modern game in that the walls were used as surfaces from which to ricochet the ball into the opponent's court.

The summer resort town of St. Andrews, Scotland, is famous for its golf courses. This map shows the elaborate—and challenging—plan of the courses.

1770, which popularized the rules of racing and printed a schedule of events. It was during this period, moreover, that sportsmen recognized the importance of proper training and physical conditioning for the winning performance of racehorses. The same sort of organization and evolution also occurred for the bat-and-ball game of cricket. All classes participated in this game, which outgrew its peasant background of stoolball around 1700. Cricket matured in the 19th century (and will be discussed later), but basic principles emerged in the 18th century. The idea was to protect a goal, called a wicket, with a bat, while a bowler tried to hit it with a hard ball about the size of an orange. It was at first popular in the southern counties and then spread to London where the Marylebone Cricket Club formed in 1787 to establish rules of play and proper etiquette.

To the north, in Scotland, golf emerged as an upper-class game in which leather balls stuffed with boiled feathers and clubs of bent thorn tree branches were used. The word *golf* comes from the Scots word *colf,* which meant club, or stick. The object was to take the least number of strokes to hit the ball into a small hole located on a green area at the end of a long fairway, or grassy stretch. In 1754 the Royal and Ancient Golf Club at St. Andrews formed to carry out the same role for golf as the Marylebone Cricket Club did for its sport. St. Andrews introduced rules, and in 1764 set 18 as the official number of holes.

In the 17th century, the Dutch launched sailing races; the word *yacht* comes from the Dutch word *jaghtschip,* which means "hunting ship" or "fast pirate ship." In Ireland

wealthy Anglo-Irishmen established the Cork Water Club in 1720 for sailing exercises, and changed their name to the Royal Cork Yacht Club in 1765. In England, after a number of changes, an exclusive club for upper-class sailors appeared in 1820, the Royal Yacht Club in London. Because the sport required leisure time and money, competitive sailing remained a pastime of the rich.

At the same time boxing evolved as a sport in which the lower classes participated, but that was enjoyed by upper-class spectators and gamblers. James Figg, an illiterate young man, opened a school for the "manly art of self-

An 18th-century golfer plays at St. Andrews.

defense" in London in the early years of the 18th century. Figg taught others to use swords, fists, and cudgels (stout sticks) for personal defense. He offered demonstrations and opportunities for making bets on contests with students at his exhibition hall. There was room for several hundred spectators sitting around a raised circular stage, the "ring."

In 1727 a pipemaker from Greenwich, Ned Sutton, challenged Figg personally. Even the king of England, George I, joined the crowd to see Figg take apart his opponent. Figg opened a cut on Sutton's shoulder with a sword, knocked Sutton down with his fists, and shattered Sutton's knee with a cudgel. Figg retired as a rich man at age 36, and his teaching was taken up by others. One of his pupils, Jack Broughton, became the best boxer in England. During a grueling match in 1741, Broughton struck his opponent below the heart. The other man collapsed and died. Distraught, Broughton devised a set of rules to reduce the brutality of boxing and separate it from wrestling.

The so-called Broughton Rules lasted more than a century—no more wrestling, no hitting below the belt or when a man was down, a 30-second rest period after a knockdown. The rules thus introduced the idea of rounds, although they were not regularly spaced and could last as long as the fighters were upright. Following a knockdown, the fighters had to "come up to scratch," a line at the center of the ring, to continue the contest. Gloves were used only in practice. After losing a match when he was 46, Broughton retired, but he was honored at his death in 1789 with burial at Westminster Abbey

in the company of famous soldiers, aristocrats, politicians, and poets.

Sports history in 18th-century Great Britain anticipated many of the aspects of modern sports. Cricket, golf, horse racing, boxing, and sailing evolved from traditional settings, but demonstrated a distinct trend toward organization and rule making. During the Industrial Revolution, which began in Britain around 1775 and continued for a century, inventors and businessmen applied rational, organized thought to their work. Although often inspired by the desire for fair gambling, this same thoughtful organization was applied to sports. The establishment of the Jockey Club of London, Marylebone Cricket Club, Royal and Ancient Golf Club of St. Andrews, Royal Cork Yacht Club, and the Broughton Rules demonstrates a growing interest in regulation and control. What happened within Great Britain was transitional to the modern era, and reflective of the new conditions developing in Western civilization.

Another aspect of this sports evolution involves the activity of Europeans in the rest of the world. In the first part of the 15th century, Europeans, equipped with ships and guns, began to explore the earth. The Portuguese traveled the coast of Africa, ventured across the Arabian Sea, through the Malacca Strait, and on to Japan. Sailing under the colors of Spain, Christopher Columbus cruised the Caribbean and opened up a New World. Ferdinand Magellan, with a fragile wooden fleet of five Spanish ships, set off on a sailing journey around the world, which was completed by his second in command, Juan Sebastian del Cano. These explorations were followed

by the journeys of settlers and merchants, and wherever the Europeans traveled they carried with them their ideas of religion, business, government, technology, and culture. With them also went their thoughts about leisure and recreation.

In North America the frontier was generally a westward-moving line of European settlement that began with the founding of the first colonies in the early 17th century and lasted until the end of the 19th century. Sports and recreation usually reflected the skills of frontier life as well as the heritage of the migrants. There was little time, however, for anything but working for survival. For example, when the Pilgrims, who were a part of the larger Puritan movement in England, settled at Plymouth in Massachusetts, the colonists worked even on Christmas Day. On December 25, 1621, a new shipload of immigrants wanted to stay home. The governor William Bradford told them that they could remain in the village if it were a matter of conscience, or religious devotion. The rest of the village population trudged off to labor on in the fields, but when they returned at noon they felt tricked. The governor found the new people "in the street at play, openly; some pitching the bar, and some at stool-ball and such like sports." The governor ended the play and everyone went to work that afternoon.

In America as well as in England, Puritans generally opposed sports. They connected sports with gambling, an explicit sin, and thought sports diverted people from godliness. Instead of allowing such recreation to continue on Sunday afternoons as had been the village custom, Puritans insisted that all of Sunday be devoted to private and public worship. There was no time for sports or games. Such recreation was idleness, considered among the worst of sins. Wrestling and shooting contests were exceptions, however, because they prepared men for military action. James I (1566–1625) and Charles I (1600–49) of England both supported Sunday afternoon recreation before the Puritans gained control of the country, lopped off the head of the king, and suppressed sports. After restoring the monarchy in 1660, Charles II revived sports activity.

In America, however, the Puritan disapproval lasted well into the 19th century and became part of an attitude that sports were frivolous. As John Adams (1735–1826), the second President of the United States commented, "I was not sent to this world to spend my days in sports, diversions and pleasures. I was born for business; for both

activity and study." Life was indeed serious at that time.

Outside the circle of New England Puritanism, however, other immigrant groups enjoyed sporting activity. In the early 18th century, William Byrd of Westover wrote in his secret diary about running, cricket, wrestling, and cudgel fights in Virginia. The Dutch at New Netherlands (New York) enjoyed boat racing, horse racing, ice skating, and skittles (ninepin bowling). At festivals they competed at gander pulls in which a live goose was tied upside down from a tree branch. The head and neck were greased, and then people on horseback galloping underneath tried to pull off the head. The person who succeeded got to keep and eat the goose. They also played "clubbing the cat," whereby an unfortunate house cat was enclosed in a small barrel that was strung between two posts. People

The Cock Pit, *an engraving by English artist William Hogarth, depicts cockfighting in 18th-century England. The sport has been banned in much of the world today.*

took turns throwing a club at the barrel until it fell apart. The person who broke the barrel and the person who caught the crazed cat afterward received prizes.

Almost everywhere, the frontiersmen competed in target shooting, wood chopping, and blood sports. John James Audubon, the great bird artist of America, described rifle contests that involved driving nails into wood with the bullet, turkeys used as targets, and "barking" a squirrel. "Barking" was done by a marksman hitting the bark of a tree near a squirrel so that the concussion, not the bullet, killed it. Cockfighting attracted all classes for gambling purposes. Roosters naturally fight to the death with wings, beak, and claws when thrown together in a small ring. After a brief, furious fight of blood and ripped feathers, the winner lives to fight another day while the loser goes home to the stew pot. Cockfighting has been banned in much of the world today, but is still legal in some places, such as the Philippines.

Rough and tumble fighting between men, something like the ancient Greek pankration, also occurred on the American frontier. Thomas Ashe, an Irish traveler, reported an early 19th-century fight between a Virginian and Kentuckian near the Ohio River:

> Very few rounds had taken place before the Virginian . . . pitched himself into the bosom of his opponent. . . . The Virginian never lost his hold; fixing his claws in his hair and his thumbs on his eyes, gave them an instantaneous start from their sockets. The sufferer roared aloud, but uttered no complaint. The Kentuckian not being able to disentangle his adversary from

his face, adopted a new mode of warfare. He extended his arms around the Virginian, and hugged him into closer contact with his huge body. The latter, disliking this, made one further effort and fastening on the under lip of his mutilator tore it over the chin. The Kentuckian at length gave out, on which the people carried off the victor . . . as the first rough and tumbler.

The Spanish in South America and Mexico introduced bullfighting shortly after the conquest of Mexico by Cortés. The history of bullfighting is vague, but bull games go back to the Minoans in 1500 B.C.E., and fights with wild animals, including bulls, were a Roman pastime. Iberia, the peninsula of Spain and Portugal, was once under Roman control and presumedly bullfights started in Spain at that time. Suppressed by Christians, bullfighting was restored in Spain by the Moors in the 8th century. At this point the fighting was done on horseback, and it was not until 1725 that Francisco Romero, a bullfighter of common origin, used a sword to kill a bull while on foot. Bullfighting became a national sport for Spain and Latin America. The Portuguese continued to fight on horseback and spared the life of the bull.

To outsiders the bullfight appears to be a cruel blood sport. To insiders, however, a bullfight is a drama, an art, in which the matador, the bullfighter, is supposed to win and the bull is required to die. It symbolizes the conquest and victory of humanity over brute force. In Latin cities on both sides of the Atlantic, arenas were built for bullfighting shows as the Spanish frontier progressed.

In northern Mexico and into the American Southwest, Spaniards established cattle

ranches in the 17th and 18th centuries. During the 19th century, as the American people moved onto the Great Plains, cowboys rounded up cattle, branded them, and drove them long distances northward out of Texas to cowtowns such as Abilene and Dodge City, Kansas. American cowboys learned to handle cattle from their Spanish predecessors, the *vaqueros,* and adapted the equipment of the Spaniard. Even the Texas longhorn cattle were originally of Spanish stock. For the Spanish as well as for the Americans, cattle raising on the plains was a frontier activity.

The work required special skills of roping, herding, tying and branding cows, and breaking wild horses for saddle work. From those skills arose the sport of rodeo. Quite naturally, when they met, cowboys tested their skills against one another. On July 4, 1864, Prescott, Arizona, which had been a town for only two months, hosted a rodeo. In 1888 Prescott staged the first professional rodeo when the citizens built a grandstand, sold tickets, and awarded silver belt buckles to the winners. William F. Cody's Buffalo Bill show, which started in 1882, popularized cowboy skills, and the July 4th holiday developed into a traditional rodeo time in the West. This time became known as the "Cowboy Christmas," because it was a day when cowboys could earn some extra money by winning prizes.

Ongoing international shows such as Cheyenne Frontier Days in 1896, the Pendleton Round-Up of Oregon in 1910, and the Calgary Stampede in 1912 were developed. Rodeo promoters formed the Rodeo Association of America in 1929 to make rules and sanction contests. The riders formed their own organization in 1936, first called the Cowboys Turtle Association, and then the Professional Rodeo Cowboys Association after 1945. Timed events became standard: bronc riding, bull and steer riding, calf and steer roping, steer wrestling, and wild cow milking. Women participated in rodeos from the beginning, but suffered exclusion in the 1940s due to a restructuring of rodeo shows to feature cowboy movie stars. In 1948 the cowgirls

Cowboy Phillip Earring rides a rodeo horse named Fiddle Face at the Cheyenne River Annual Rodeo in South Dakota in the early 1900s.

The 1880s saw women bowling their afternoons away dressed in the height of fashion. The floor-length dresses almost certainly affected their freedom of movement.

formed the Girls Rodeo Association (after 1967 called the Women's Professional Rodeo Association), which was able to get barrel racing accepted as a regular part of rodeo events.

The American frontier, which created rodeo, moved westward across the United States until pioneers filled the land. Meanwhile, in the settled, eastern portions of the country, a notable, but loosely joined group of men called "the fancy" influenced the development of modern sports. In 19th-century America, and also England, a subculture emerged that challenged the restrictive morality of the time. The fancy liked to gamble, drink, smoke, go to parties, and attend sporting events. The word *fan* as a synonym for a spectator may have come from the name "fancy." There is also the opinion that "fan" comes from the word *fanatic*, as a description of spectator attitude.

The fancy spent their spare time bowling and playing billiards in saloons. The term *alley* used in bowling comes from the custom of setting up bowling lanes in the alleyways beside or behind the taverns. Billiard games were especially popular. In 1859 Michael Phelan beat John Seereiter in a championship at Fireman Hall in Detroit after an all-night game. Phelan won $10,000 in a bet with Seereiter, and $5,000 more from the promoter of the event, who had sold 500 seats to fans. Phelan, who owned a New York billiard parlor and manufactured tables, promoted the game by forming the American Billiard Players Association in 1865. Although wealthy people often installed their own private tables, the game never quite lost its disreputable association with saloons and bars. For most people in the 19th century the billiard table, and later the pool table, were symbols of dissipation. John Quincy Adams, who donated a billiard table to the White House while he was President, for instance, was unfairly accused by his opponents in the 1828 election of installing gambling equipment at public expense.

The restless fancy liked almost any sporting event that provided an opportunity to gamble. By the 1850s sports halls catered to their interests, and Frederick Van Wyck, a member of the New York City aristocracy, commented that attendance at these events was a rite of passage for young men of the upper classes. Going to Tommy Norris's livery stable, Van Wyck reported witnessing a cockfight, a goat fight, a boxing match between two women who were nude above the waist, and a "ratting," in which people bet on how long it took a terrier to kill all the rats in a pit. "Certainly for a lad of 17, such as I," he said, "a night with Tommy Norris and his attractions was quite a night."

Philip Hone, another rich, upper-class New Yorker, kept a detailed diary that included comments about sporting events in the city. Like other people of the time he frowned on sports as useless, but at the same time he was fascinated by them. On Friday, April 24, 1835, he observed a 10-mile run at a horse-racing track on Long Island. John Cox Stevens and Samuel L. Gouverneur, both wealthy men of New York, had made a bet about whether or not a man could run 10 miles in less than an hour. Stevens offered a prize of $1,000 for the person who could do it. Hone joined the noisy, dusty crowd of 20,000 at the track, sniffed with disapproval at the great amount of betting, and watched as nine men started the race. Five of the runners made the first five miles in 30 minutes, but only three finished the race. Wearing black pantaloons and flesh-colored slippers, the winner, Henry Stannard of Connecticut, was the only person to cover the distance in less than an hour. He finished in 59 minutes 48 seconds, a six-minute-per-mile pace. Hone commented that Stannard was tall and thin. "He appeared to me exactly of the size and form for such an undertaking, with much bone and muscle and very little fat. He was not distressed by his effort," wrote Hone.

At this time, running was called "pedestrianism." Random athletic events were organized by people like Stevens for entertainment and gambling. They occurred during the period when modern sports were starting to form and involved many of the elements that still sustain modern athletics: organization, urbanization, a quest for a record and the tools of statistical measurement to confirm records, leisure, a venue for performance, transportation systems, newspapers for publicity, athletes willing to perform, and gambling. These conditions were created in large part by the Industrial Revolution.

Beginning in Great Britain about 1775 and lasting for a century, British merchants with money left over from trade began to invest in textile factories and coal mines. Mechanical inventions and new technology made the work more efficient and provided cheaper products of higher quality. Overall, the Industrial Revolution made possible a higher standard of living for the British people. They had more money, better places to live, more clothing, and time for something besides work. The Industrial Revolution also prompted people to move from the countryside to the cities where the factories were located. Inventions for agriculture, at the same time, allowed farmers to produce more food with less labor to meet the needs of the ever-increasing urban population.

For the people packed into the cities, there was both an opportunity, and a need, for sports entertainment and participation. A pedestrian event, like that of Stevens, provided something to talk about and see. It enriched urban life and created a diversion from the often boring work of industry and business. With a lag of about 25 years behind Great Britain, the United States experienced its own industrial revolution with many of the same consequences. It is interesting that Hone encountered a great crowd of men and boys at the race track on Long Island on a Friday afternoon. At a time when most people regularly worked every day except Sunday, the attraction of such sporting events was impressive.

The fancy also liked boxing. It was a sport ready-made for gambling and easy to stage. The first professional black American boxer, Tom Molyneux from Virginia, supposedly fought his way out of slavery with his fists after his master matched him against another slave. He gained a reputation for fighting among the fancy of New York City, and traveled to England in 1810 to face the British champion, Tom Cribb. In the fight, Molyneux knocked Cribb out in the 31st round, but tripped, hit the ring post, and became insensible. Both men revived and fought on until the 40th round, when Cribb knocked Molyneux unconscious. At a rematch in 1811 before 40,000 fans, Cribb broke Molyneux's jaw in the 10th round and knocked him out in the 11th. After this Molyneux drifted into the English backcountry and made a sparse living giving demonstrations of boxing. He died penniless and alcoholic in 1821. Cribb became a saloon owner, and his pub still exists near the National Gallery in London.

Philip Hone, who was critical of the fancy, recorded impressions about these illegal boxing matches in his diary:

> One of these infamous meetings took place yesterday [September 13, 1842] on the bank of the North River in Westchester. . . . Two men, named Lilly and McCoy, thumped and battered each other for the gratification of a brutal gang of spectators, until the latter after 119 rounds fell dead in the ring. . . . McCoy went into the battle, it is said, expressing a determination to conquer or to die. He was deficient in science, but a bulldog in courage. The fight lasted two hours and forty-three minutes. McCoy received one hundred square blows and was knocked down eighty-one times.

During the 1840s and 1850s prizefighting became enormously popular in the United States. John "Old Smoke" Morrissey's story is a tale of "rags to riches." He came to the United States as a three-year-old from Ireland in a family of eight children. He grew up as a street fighter, moved to New York City from Troy, New York, and announced his arrival by challenging all comers to a free-for-all fight at the Empire Club saloon. He was promptly beaten to a pulp. He recovered, worked for Tammany Hall, a political organization, and scrapped in minor prizefights. After failing to find gold in the California gold rush, he returned to New York and in 1853 beat Yankee Sullivan for the unofficial American championship. He invested his $2,000 winnings in a gambling house that became the most famous in the city by 1860. In 1857 he defeated a challenger, John C. Heenan, and retired from the ring. Morrissey expanded his gambling operations to Saratoga, New York, and went into a lottery business. He was elected to Congress in 1866 and 1868, and died with fortune and fame in 1878.

Heenan, meanwhile, assumed the championship and went about giving demonstrations. In 1860 he fought Tom Sayers, the English champion, outside of London. The bout attracted great interest on both sides of the Atlantic, with British aristocrats joining the riffraff to enjoy a two-

This painting depicts the prize fight between Tom Sayers (left) and John Heenan in 1860. After two hours of fighting, referees called the bout a draw.

hour bloodbath. Heenan was 6 feet 1 inch tall and weighed 190 pounds; Sayers was 5 feet 8 inches tall and weighed 160. In the seventh round Sayers pulled a muscle, or perhaps broke a bone in his right arm, but continued to fight. Finally, with both fighters exhausted and bloody and the crowd out of control, someone cut the ropes of the ring and the referee called the fight a draw.

For all of their brutality and devotion to pleasure, the fancy played an important role in America and England. Looking for excitement, wealthy people began to promote sporting events. This helped overcome the disapproval of recreation that reached back to the Puritans and allowed society to accept sporting activity. William Lyon Phelps, a professor at Yale, for instance, reported reading the news of the day in 1892 to his father, a Baptist minister. "I had never heard him mention a prize fight and did not suppose he knew anything on the subject, or cared anything about it. So when I came to the headline CORBETT DEFEATS SULLIVAN, I read that aloud and turned the page. My father leaned forward and said earnestly, 'Read it by rounds!'"

John Cox Stevens and James Gordon Bennett, Jr., were the most important Americans involved in the transition. They were both rich and interested in competition. Stevens (1785–1857) was the son of a New Jersey inventor and heir to a steamboat fortune. He married into the New York upper class and lived a life of constant parties, dances, and excursions. He loved horse racing and in 1823 bet heavily—his purse, watch, and diamond stickpin—on the horse, American Eclipse, to win the "Race of the Century." This was a challenge match between American Eclipse, the fastest horse of the North, and Sir Henry, the fastest horse of the South. Charged with the excitement of sectional rivalry between North and South in the United States, 50,000 fans watched the event at the Union racetrack on Long Island. American Eclipse beat Sir Henry in two out of three four-mile races and afterward Stevens bought both horses for his personal stables.

In 1831, Stevens established a center for sports clubs on a part of his family estate at Hoboken, New Jersey, across the river from New York City. The Elysian Fields,

The *America's* Cup: "His head shall replace the trophy"

It stands 2 feet 3 inches high, weighs 8 pounds 6 ounces, and is the oldest existing international trophy in sports. It was originally called the "Hundred Guinea Cup" and cost $510. After winning it in 1851, the syndicate that built the winning yacht, *America,* gave the cup to the New York Yacht Club as a prize for international sailing. The club displayed it in a special case, and there was a legend that if any American should ever lose the competition his head would replace the trophy in the empty case.

The various competitions of this most exclusive of sports have been subject to rule changes and protests. Until 1927 any size vessel could be used to race, and from 1958 to 1987 only 12-meter yachts were allowed (measurement involves a complicated formula using length of the boat at the water line, sail area, and height). The rules have been subject to court challenge, and in 1988 the United States beat New Zealand using a catamaran, or double-hull design. It was a gross mismatch.

Protests have been frequent. In 1934, after losing a dispute about the proper raising of a protest flag, a British journalist commented that "Britannia rules the waves, but America waives the rules."

The race has been held irregularly, with intervals from one to 21 years, but recently the race has been held every 4 years. In 1983, the 26th competition, Australia beat the United States in the best four of seven races. It was the first time the Americans had lost the cup.

The Australians used a radical, winged keel under their boat, *Australia II.* Captain John Bertrand commented, "*Australia II* did not merely turn, or even turn fast. She whipped around . . . she spun tight and fast, her winged keel magically almost on a dime." The Aussies came to the dock singing "Waltzing Matilda," one of their national songs, while the American captain, Dennis Conner, wondered about his head. Conner survived and recovered the cup while sailing for the San Diego Yacht Club during the Australian races in 1987. He lost it again, however, in 1995 to a team from New Zealand in the 30th competition.

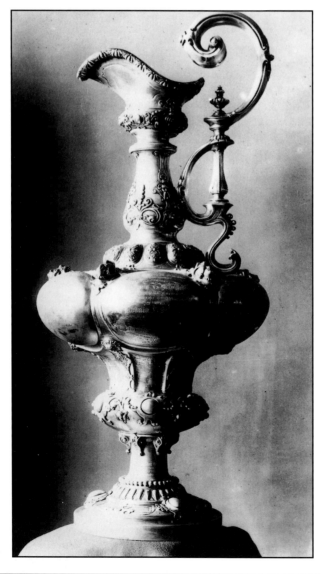

The America's *Cup was won by the United States in all but 2 of the 30 competitions held from 1851 to 1995.*

as it was called, became a retreat for the rich. Headquarters for the New York Yacht Club, St. George Cricket Club, and New York Athletic Club were constructed there. Stevens became the first "commodore" (president) of the New York Yacht Club, which hosted dinners featuring turtle soup, cruises along the coast, and an annual regatta (boat races) at Newport, Rhode Island. The regatta was the highlight of the New York social season.

With others, Stevens constructed a special $30,000 racing yacht, *America*, that competed against 17 British boats 58 miles around the Isle of Wight in the English Channel. The race was a part of the London Exposition of 1851, and at first no one would face the fast *America* with its sharp bow and slanted masts. The Royal Yacht Club donated a cup, however, and after Stevens and his crew won the race Queen Victoria graciously visited the boat to congratulate the winners. In 1857, the year of Stevens's death, the winners gave the trophy to the New York Yacht Club as a prize for international sailing competition. In all but 2 of the 30 competitions that have taken place from 1851 to 1995, the United States retained possession of the prize, which has become known as the *America*'s Cup. This trophy is the oldest prize for an international sailing competition.

Following Stevens as a rich patron of sports was a younger colleague, James Gordon Bennett, Jr. (1841–1918). He inherited wealth from his Scots father, who was the owner of the *New York Herald* newspaper. At age 16 he became a member of the New York Yacht Club and owner of a 77-foot vessel. Given to brash acts, he won the first

transatlantic sailing race and $60,000 in bets in 1866 by braving a violent storm that washed six crewmen overboard to their deaths. In 1875, after watching polo in England, he brought mallets, balls, and a coach to the United States to teach his rich friends at Newport how to play. He brought cow ponies, horses noted for their agility, from Texas and started the Westchester Polo Club in New York.

Bennett gave a boost to tennis in America after he was thrown out of the Reading Room, a snobbish social club at Newport in 1878. Bennett dared an English friend to ride a horse into the lobby of the club and after the man did so the outraged members of the Reading Room withdrew Bennett's membership. He then built a sports complex called the Casino a few blocks away. The national tennis championships were held there from 1881 to 1914. Bennett, however, went to live in Paris, France, in 1878. In Europe, he continued to support sports by providing trophies for auto and balloon racing, contributing to the Olympic movement, and reporting sports events in his New York newspaper.

Despite their sometimes unseemly actions, the fancy publicized and financed sports during a period of much popular censure. Their actions introduced new sports, and their positions of prominence brought grudging approval of athletic competition from the upper class. The clubs they established for their own pleasure helped give definition and regulation to sports. Most important, they helped to change the attitudes of an industrial society that desperately needed new sources of recreation and entertainment.

James Gordon Bennett, heir to the New York Herald *newspaper fortune, was a proponent of sailing and tennis, and brought polo to the United States from England in 1875.*

Chapter 4

The Sports of Empire

The discoveries of science and the technology of the Industrial Revolution gave power and influence to Western civilization. Westerners could travel upstream against river currents in steamboats; communicate instantly via telegraphs and telephones; and move overland quickly on railroads. Quinine gave them immunity to malaria in Africa, and machine guns provided a way to defeat vast armies of native peoples armed only with spears. A "new" imperialism in the last part of the 19th century resulted in the domination of Africa, India, and Asia by Western nations. The newcomers took with them into the world not only their dominating technology, but also their culture, which included their athletics. Those who were defeated by the West paid attention and often imitated the sports of the conquerors.

The 19th century is sometimes referred to as the "British Century" because of the growth and strength of Great Britain. The British Empire was so vast and so spread around the world that it was said the sun never set on it. Wherever they went the British took their sports, which they believed were important. Reverend J. E. C.

Welldon, headmaster of Harrow School from 1881–95, commented, "In the history of the British Empire it is written that England has owed her sovereignty to her sports." It was an idea that was fervently believed. The duke of Wellington (1769–1852), who defeated Napoleon, probably never said, "The battle of Waterloo was won on the playing fields of Eton," but it was nonetheless a thought that was firmly believed. As historian Allen Guttmann concluded in his 1994 book *Games and Empires*, "From the remnants of wickets and bats, future archaeologists of material culture will be able to reconstruct the boundaries of the British Empire."

With direction from the Marylebone Cricket Club (MCC) of London, cricket was well developed by the time of the new imperialism. It evolved from village games in southern and eastern England and became the first team sport in which upper-class players exercised themselves without the use of a horse. Lord's in London, the premier playing field (or "pitch" as it is called) improved as spectator interest grew in the 1860s. Groundsmen began to smooth out the rough surface, especially the area of

With his cap pulled low over his eyes and the ball tucked safely away, England's goalkeeper, Frank Swift, leaps past the feet of Scotsman Laurie Reilly. In this soccer match, held at Wembley Stadium in London, the underdog Scottish team defeated the English team 3-1.

By 1865, cricket had become an integral part of English life. Britain's 19th-century imperialism helped spread the sport around the world.

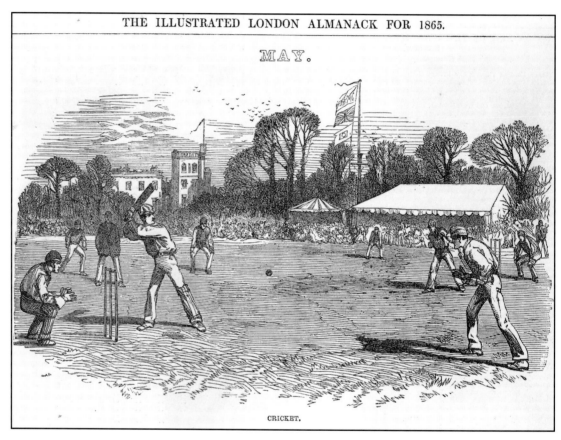

THE ILLUSTRATED LONDON ALMANACK FOR 1865.

MAY.

CRICKET.

the "wicket," where the ball was thrown. This was important because the pitched ball normally bounced off the ground before reaching the batsman. Rope boundaries and stands were set up for a game between Eton and Harrow in 1866.

Rules written by the MCC in 1835 required an underhanded pitch, but a quicker overhand throw became popular and the rules changed to allow it in 1864. Still, the ball had to be delivered in a smooth motion, so a stiff, overhanded style with a short run developed. Cricket was played on a large oval field with the action in the center on a rectangular wicket area, 10 feet wide by 22 yards long. On each end in a "crease" portion stood upright wickets, three closely spaced stumps poked into the ground with two bails, or wooden blocks, balanced

between the tops. If the area was wet, playing was difficult and the condition was called a "sticky wicket."

Each side had 11 players, and after 10 outs the sides switched. The job of the batsman was to protect the wicket and hit the ball. When hit in any direction, if the batter could reach the opposite crease, he scored a run. The bowler then switched ends and continued to throw against the same batter until he was out. Scoring a "century," or 100 runs, was considered a worthy accomplishment. An out could be made by knocking off the bails with the pitch, catching the batted ball before it hit the ground, or knocking off the bails while the batter was running. The defensive men scattered in all directions on the field and caught the hard, red ball with bare hands.

The distinctive manner of dress, with all-white shirts and trousers topped with round, narrow-brimmed caps, evolved in the 1860s and 1870s.

Cricket became an integral part of English life for both men and women, and almost every village or town had its cricket pitch. Games were slow, and matches, especially championships, could last as long as five days, with time out for tea, lunch, supper, and sleep. George Bernard Shaw (1856–1950), the Irish playwright, said that cricket had been invented to give the English, "who are not a very spiritual people," some idea of eternity.

Rugby and soccer (called football everywhere but in the United States) developed as faster, rougher sports. Modern soccer was an adaptation of the earlier ball games of medieval England and France. Schools in 19th-century England developed their own brands of soccer, such as the Eton "wall game," in which 20 boys on each team shoved and kicked to move a ball along a 120-yard brick wall toward a small garden door at one end or a tree stump at the other. At Rugby School, where there were open fields, the boys developed a game of kicking and running that featured massive team scrums (clumped struggles) with pushing and hacking (kicking in the shins). In general, the intention of such ball games was to move a ball across a line or into a goal of some sort.

Rugby published its rules in 1845. In 1848, 14 representatives of various English colleges met to work out common rules so they could play one another. An argument ensued with Eton screaming at Rugby about running with the ball. Rugby rules were not accepted. The argument was settled in 1863 by the new Football Association in London, which banned tripping, hacking, holding, pushing, throwing the ball, and passing the ball. The name "Football Association" was shortened to "Assoc," from which came the term *soccer*. Soccer thus started as a middle-class, schoolboy pastime rooted in medieval football games. It spread quickly as clubs formed in churches and factories. The Football Association reluctantly opened its doors to these outside groups in 1888. Soccer, consequently, became a "people's game" with a strong link to the working class, regardless of the intention of the founders.

Rugby went its own way, and in 1871 the Rugby Football Union was formed. The organization abolished hacking, limited the size of teams to 15 members on the field, and assigned points for touchdowns when the ball passed the end line, and field goals when it was kicked between goalposts. In the 1880s new rules opened the game up to lateral passes and downfield running maneuvers. The slugging, mauling scrum was retained, but minimized in use. Rugby remained largely an elite schoolboy sport of the middle and upper classes.

Both soccer and cricket traveled overseas, carried by Englishmen and buoyed by the enthusiastic expansion of the new imperialism. In Australia, where the majority of the population came from Britain, cricket was played without the lower-class exclusions found in England. Army and navy garrisons formed clubs in Sydney in 1826, followed by other groups in Melbourne and Adelaide. The sport became a part of school curriculum for both boys and girls,

British and U.S. naval officers play a match of cricket at the Potomac Park Polo Grounds near Washington, D.C., in 1930. On the right, C. K. T. Wheen of the U.S. hits the ball while J. M. Branch of Britain looks on from behind the wicket.

and international competition with England began in 1861.

In 1873–74 the great W. G. Grace, England's best player, toured Australia with a team, and two members remained behind to coach in Sydney and Melbourne. It gave a sense of pride for the "colonials" to beat the homeland at their own game, and Australia sent a team to London. They beat the Marylebone Cricket Club on their own pitch in 1878. When another touring Australian team won in 1882, the London *Sporting Times* lamented the death of English cricket and jokingly said that the body should be cremated with the ashes taken to Australia. A group of Melbourne women subsequently burned a

bail, put the ashes in an urn, and gave it to the English captain. This started a biannual rivalry to win the "Ashes."

The competition was usually friendly, but in 1932–33 the Marylebone Cricket Club sent a team to tour Australia captained by Douglas R. Jardine, who believed his team should intimidate the batsman. He and others threw sharply bouncing bowls aimed at the upper body and unprotected head. When the batter protected himself with the bat the weakly hit ball could be easily fielded. This was called the "bodyline assault." After two Australian batsmen were "beaned" by straight-thrown balls, the Australian newspapers complained that it was "not cricket," and the Australian Cricket Board sent a telegram to Marylebone complaining of unsportsmanlike play. The Marylebone Cricket Club felt insulted, and the matter had to be settled by diplomats. The world was in the depths of the Great Depression, and the unity of the empire was more important than the "ashes."

In the former British colonies in the West Indies, cricket meant more than beating the homeland. It was an opportunity for racial integration—a time for whites and blacks, former masters and slaves, to compete on equal terms. The all-white Caribbean clubs recruited talented blacks when it came time to face a strong team from the homeland. The clubs retained the honored position of captain for a white until 1960 when Frank Worrell was elected to lead the West Indian team against the English and Australians. V. S. Naipaul, the novelist who was born in Trinidad in 1932, commented that minorities in the islands had known mainly greed and brutality.

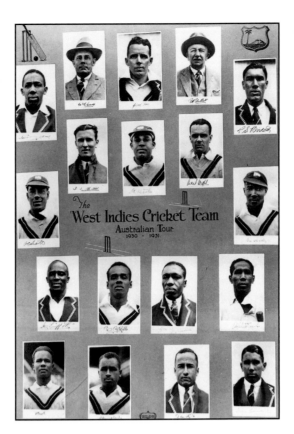

Members of the West Indian cricket team from 1930–31 during their extensive tour of Australia.

Cricket, however, with its code of fair play, provided a place where skill, courage, and grace was recognized.

The same sort of exclusion was practiced by employees of the East India Company, a worldwide British trading company, when they started playing cricket in India in 1721. The Parsees, an Indian religious group in Bombay, nonetheless, formed a team in 1848. This club and others were encouraged by English viceroys, particularly Lord Harris (George Robert Channing Harris), who started an annual tournament between British residents and the Parsees in 1892. To the shock of fellow Britons, Harris actually ate lunch with the Indians, and once claimed, "The game of cricket has done more to draw the Mother Country and the Colonies together than years of beneficial legislation could have done."

Indians educated in England also supported the game. The most famous was Prince Ranjitsinhji, Maharaja Jam Sahib of Nawangar (1872–1933), otherwise known as "Ranji." He learned to play in India, attended Cambridge University in Great Britain, and represented England in play against Australia. In 1907 Ranji returned to India to reign as a Maharaja and promote

cricket. The game appealed to the Indian princes because of its aristocratic history and association with the British rulers. It was also suitable for warm climates, where players preferred only casual exertion. By the 1930s cricket was a major urban sport in the subcontinent. Interestingly, during the break between India and Great Britain that occurred with Indian independence, those Indians educated in England argued that it was not "fair play," or "not cricket," for the British to deny them their proper chance to run their government.

The acceptance of cricket in India was hindered by the Hindu religion, which prohibited the use of leather made from cows, an animal considered sacred. Cricket balls, as well as soccer balls, were made with leather coverings. In the late 19th century, Cecil Tyndale-Briscoe, an Anglican missionary-teacher in the Kashmir, had to allow the boys at his school to catch the cricket ball with their hands covered by their sleeves. A soccer player struck in the face by the ball had to be rushed to a nearby canal, washed, and purified. Another defiled player was not allowed to return home and had to go live with relatives. Tyndale-Briscoe and other English teachers, however, were persistent and eventually gained some ground against the religious prohibition.

The diffusion of sports was not an entirely one-way affair in India. Polo, for instance, traveled in the opposite direction—from Indians to Britons. Variations of horse games had been played in Asia for centuries. The ancient Persians played a game like lacrosse on horseback, and the Afghans played *buzkashi,* in which hundreds of mounted men fought with each other to reach down, pick up, and carry a headless calf, or goat, around a pole to a target area. Mongols, supposedly, used the heads or skulls of enemies as balls to hit about in macabre horse games. In India, English cavalry officers on horseback competed in races, and in the hunting of wild boars with spears.

During the 1850s in Assam, in northeastern India, horsemen from Manipur entertained British officers by hitting a ball of willow root up and down a field with sticks. When asked, the Indians called the root-ball "pulu." The officers tried their skill at hitting the ball, but added goal posts, chose teams, and made rules for their new game of "polo." As it developed, the sport required four horsemen per side and a match divided into six periods called "chukkas," a word of Indian origin. The purpose was to hit a white wooden ball about the size of a baseball between goalposts at the ends of a 300-yard field. The players used long-handled mallets carried in the right hand and observed right-of-way rules to protect horses and riders. The British established a club in Calcutta in 1862, and from there the game spread quickly among the English cavalry and Indian royalty. It was considered good training for warfare.

The first polo demonstration in England occurred in 1870 with a match at Hounslow Heath between the 10th Hussars and the 9th Lancers—a meeting noted more for strong language than for strong play. James Gordon Bennett, Jr., observed the sport in England and took it to the United States in 1875 for his upper-class friends. English army officers transported the sport to West and South Africa, and immigrants of British descent installed it in Argentina. There polo became an important part of the military tradition, with the result that Buenos Aires evolved as the main center of polo activity in the 20th century.

Meanwhile, during the 1860s and 1870s, soccer spread from English schools to Belgium, Holland, France, Switzerland, and Germany. It was taken up at first by schoolboys and taught by transplanted Englishmen, or people acquainted with English schools. During the early 1880s, Britons and Germans started clubs for young adults in Germany, and the game began to follow the same path as in England. Soccer became the passionate sport of the working class. During the 1880s, British sailors introduced soccer into Italy, British merchants organized the first clubs, and Italian businessmen brought soccer balls home from trips to England.

In 1903–4, Robert Guerin organized in France the Fédération Internationale de Football Association (FIFA) for international soccer play. At first the British groups, snootily thinking that it was their game, refused to participate in FIFA. They did join the charter members France, Belgium,

Denmark, Holland, Spain, and Sweden two years later. FIFA became the largest and most important of all the international sports federations.

In their scramble to dominate Africa in the latter part of the 19th century, the European nations took their sports with them. None of the nations, however, played with zeal equal to the English. The history of sports in Africa is not well known, but the Union of South Africa started a Football Association in 1892 as did Kenya in 1922. Prejudiced French colonists tried unsuccessfully to prevent African players from using shoes to play soccer in the French Congo in the 1920s. In that area it was thought by the native peoples that each team started with a god-given number of goals. Magicians battled beforehand to steal points, and the actual game only acted out what had been determined by the magic. In

Tunisia and Algeria, Islamic countries ruled by the French, soccer became a sport of resistance. Arab rebels used sports clubs as places to meet in order to plot political upheaval and used sports victories to undermine French colonial power. Their thought was that if Arabs could win at soccer, they could win at warfare. At least, it was good publicity for the Arabs.

The 75,000 British soldiers in India played soccer and other sports for fitness and morale. Service in the subcontinent was hot and tedious. As one old trooper, quoted in the May 1990 issue of *The International Journal of the History of Sport*, put it, "We had one great weapon against boredom. The answer was sport, sport, sport." Competitive clubs formed in Calcutta and elsewhere in the late 19th century. By 1900 the large open area in front of Fort William in the center of Calcutta, the Maidan,

The U.S. Army polo team takes on the British Army team (in the dark jerseys) in 1923. King George and Queen Mary viewed the match, which was held at Hurlingham, England, and won by the Americans, 8-4.

which was there to provide a clear field of fire in case of attack, had changed into a sports area with tennis courts, golf course, riding roads, cricket pitches, and soccer fields. In 1911 a native Bengali soccer team, Mohan Bagan, defeated the East Yorkshire Regiment team before a crowd estimated at 50,000-60,000. The Indians, of course, celebrated this victory over their masters, and the British had the opportunity to show restrained good sportsmanship.

In Latin America soccer became important in the last half of the 19th century as British merchants, British schools, and railroad workers played and started clubs. Alexander Watson Hutton from Scotland, for example, joined the faculty of St. Andrew's College in Buenos Aires in 1881. Three years later, he opened an English high school, which included a soccer field for boys and tennis courts for girls. When his imported soccer balls arrived, puzzled customs officials listed them as "items for the crazy English." The game, nonetheless, flourished and in 1893 Hutton organized the Argentine Football Association. The group changed to a Spanish name in 1905, but Hutton was remembered as the "father of Argentine soccer."

Elsewhere in Latin America—Uruguay, Guatemala, Chile, Brazil, Mexico—the pattern was similar. In Uruguay, teams sprouted along the railroad lines, and Uruguay won team championships in the 1924 and 1928 Olympics. In 1930, Uruguay won the first FIFA World Cup against Argentina. In Brazil, Charles Miller, born in Sao Paulo and educated in England, returned from abroad in 1894 with a pair of soccer balls. There were no matches, so

Miller promptly began to recruit teammates from the English railroads, banks, and utilities. By 1902 São Paulo had a soccer league, by 1914 all social classes played in Brazil, and in 1919 Brazil won the South American championship.

Unlike other South American nations, Brazil had a large African population, the result of slave importations to provide labor for sugar plantations during the colonial era. Slavery was not abolished in Brazil until 1888, but in the early 20th century Brazilian blacks began to appear on the smaller soccer teams. There was some racial prejudice, and in Rio de Janeiro the poor blacks formed their own club, Flamengo, which used a black vulture as a symbol. Over time, prejudice declined and blacks dominated the teams. Soccer became the most important of South American sports, and at São Paulo crowds of 250,000 fans gather to cheer contemporary teams.

The most famous player—perhaps the best soccer player of all time—was Edson Arantes do Nascimento, known popularly as Pelé. He led Brazil to World Cup championships in 1958, 1962, and 1970. Soccer, he said, is "the greatest joy of the people." In Brazil as elsewhere, the English sport became the "people's game." Indeed, soccer is now the world's most popular spectator sport, and the World Cup championships every four years attract intense international interest.

In North America, English settlers also brought their sports. In 1710, for example, William Byrd of Virginia wrote that he had sprained his "backside" playing cricket. Cricket continued after the American Revolution and as late as 1859 an English cricket team toured the eastern United States and Canada to play against local teams. Cricket, however, did not last. Soccer did not catch on as it had elsewhere—at least, not until the 1990s. In 19th-century North America, a variety of immigrant groups served to blunt allegiance to England and its sports. The United States had broken with Great Britain, undergone its own industrial revolution, become an international power, and followed a somewhat different sports path. Canada, a close neighbor, found the cultural energy of the United States impossible to resist and became involved in the unique sports development of the continent.

Some of the older sports of the fancy, particularly horse racing, bowling, and boxing, prospered. Blood sports, however, were suppressed. English intellectuals, supported by scientific investigations of anatomy, recognized the phenomenon of pain in animals. Jeremy Bentham (1748–1832), an English philosopher who wrote about pleasure and pain in humans, also raised the question about suffering in animals. Methodists in the 18th century opposed sports in general, and blood sports in particular, as entertainments of the devil. Urban professionals, who gained greater voting power in England in 1832, combined with the various clergymen and the Society for the Prevention of Cruelty to Animals (SPCA), to pass the Cruelty to Animals Act of 1835. After vigorous prosecution of the people involved in bull-running and cock fighting, most of the traditional blood sports in England died out during the next 15 years.

The American Society for the Prevention of Cruelty to Animals was chartered in New York in 1866 and a similar

Pelé: The Best Player of the "People's Game"

He was not very big—5 feet 8 inches—and he was not very heavy—150 pounds. Nonetheless, he excited audiences and blasted opponents' nets with dazzling ball handling. He had a sense of everyone's position on the field and the moves that a player would make. He was famous for his interceptions. Edson Arantes do Nascimento, known to soccer fans as Pelé, was born in 1940 at Tres Coracoes in northeastern Brazil. He dropped out of school in the fourth grade, and went to work as an apprentice shoemaker. His father taught him to play soccer, and the talented Pelé began playing with the major league Santos club in 1956 at age 16. "Many times, people ask me where I come from," he said. "This is a very hard question, because the answer is nothing. I come from nothing, because where I grew up in Brazil was a very poor place in the middle of nowhere. Also my nickname means nothing. Pelé. It is just a word."

He was selected to play with the Brazilian national team, and in 1958 led them to victory in the World Cup at the finals in Sweden. The fans chanted "Pelé, Pelé," and at age 16 he was world famous. Brazil won again in 1962 and 1970 with Pelé starring as the inside left forward. During his professional career, Pelé scored 1,281 goals in 1,363 games, although opponents often gave him double coverage. One of his greatest plays occurred in August 1959 in a game between Santos and Juventus, another Brazilian team. Pelé took a pass at midfield, and then went around and over various defenders without letting the ball strike the ground. At the net he faked the goaltender out of position and kicked the ball into the net for a score. Pelé retired in 1974, but returned to the field with the New York Cosmos in 1975 for two and a half years in an attempt to establish professional soccer in the United States.

Perhaps the greatest player in the history of soccer, Pelé has held every scoring record in Brazil. In international matches, he averaged one goal per game.

suppression of blood sports occurred on a state-by-state basis in the United States through the remainder of the century. By 1900, for example, most states had banned cockfighting and prizefighting as well. In order to diminish the violence of boxing, English promoters drafted the Marquis of Queensberry rules in 1867. These rules established three-minute rounds with a one-minute rest; a ten-second count for a knockout; three weight classes; use of gloves; and prohibition of punches to the kidney, back of the neck (the rabbit punch), or below the belt. There was still no limit on the number of rounds fought, however.

John L. Sullivan (1858–1918) was the last bare-knuckle champion in the United States, and the first to fight under the Marquis of Queensberry rules. Sullivan was born in Boston to Irish parents and took up prizefighting in 1878. Richard Kyle Fox, editor of the tabloid *National Police Gazette*, had begun to publicize boxing and to designate official champions. After Sullivan defeated Paddy Ryan, the first champion in 1882, Fox began a search for someone to beat the "Boston Strong Boy." Fox called Sullivan a dangerous drunk and a bully.

"The wonder is that he has never killed anyone," wrote Fox, "for he has such a terrific wallop that the head and shoulders of his victim sometimes hit the canvas before the buttocks."

Meanwhile, Sullivan toured the country and offered $1,000 to anyone who could spar with him for four rounds without being knocked out. Supposedly, only one person won the money. The publicity and his happy-go-lucky lifestyle made Sullivan a national athletic hero—the first sports celebrity in American history. Sullivan avoided worthy black boxers, defeated Fox's man Jake Kilrain in the last bare-knuckle fight in 1889, and fell in a bout against "Gentleman Jim" Corbett in 1892. The Louisiana legislature approved of gloved matches, and in 1890 the Olympic Club of New Orleans built the first modern, indoor boxing arena. The club matched Sullivan with Corbett, who had attended college, held a white-collar job as a bank clerk, and learned boxing at an elite athletic club.

Sullivan, who had been eating and drinking too much, suffered a knockout in the 21st round. He was so exhausted that he could not raise his arms to protect himself from Corbett's blows. After reviving from the knockout, the defeated champion endeared himself to the crowd at ringside: "All I have to say is that I came into the ring once too often, and if I had to get licked I'm glad I was licked by an American. I remain your warm and personal friend, John L. Sullivan." The Boston Strong Boy then retired from boxing and eventually became a popular temperance (anti-liquor) speaker.

Although Sullivan and other white champions avoided black fighters, Jack Johnson

Boxer John L. Sullivan also pursued an acting career. Advertised here is his first performance, in the play "Honest Hearts and Willing Hands."

Jack Johnson and his wife, Lucille Cameron Johnson, in Chicago in 1921. Many people were uncomfortable with their interracial marriage, and sports writers frequently called for a "great white hope" to defeat him.

(1878–1946), a black who had grown up on the docks of Galveston, Texas, found a path to the championship. He pursued the reigning champion around the world, offering challenges. Finally, in Australia in 1908, Tommy Burns agreed to fight for a guaranteed $30,000. Johnson easily won and became world champion. Johnson lived a flashy life, wearing high-fashion clothes and driving fast cars. He married a white woman, and this crossing of the color line between the races raised a national cry among sportswriters for a "great white hope" to defeat Johnson.

The champion left the United States in 1913 to avoid a prison sentence for taking a woman across a state line for immoral purposes. He traveled in Europe during World War I, ran out of money, and agreed to fight Jess Willard in Cuba in 1915. Johnson lost in the 26th round. In 1920 Johnson returned to the United States, served a one-year prison term, failed with a comeback, and then spent the rest of his life giving boxing exhibitions. He died in an automobile crash while en route to see Joe Louis fight.

Jack Dempsey (1895–1983), who came from a poor mining family in Colorado, took the championship from Willard in 1919 after knocking him down five times in the first round. Dempsey's manager, George L. "Tex" Rickard, the first major fight promoter, skillfully maneuvered Dempsey through a series of fights, including the famous fights with Gene Tunney in 1926 and 1927. In the first match, Tunney avoided Dempsey's rushes and skillfully counter-punched his way to a favorable 10th-round decision by the judges. In the second fight,

Jack Dempsey wears his trademark tigerish expression in a bout with fellow boxer Tony Fuente (in helmet) during a 1927 fight in Santa Monica, California. Proceeds from the fight benefited victims of the Mississippi flood.

Joe Louis (standing) successfully defends his heavyweight crown against Max Schmeling of Germany on June 22, 1938. To many in the U.S., Louis's victory was seen as a victory over Hitler, even though Schmeling was not a Nazi.

Dempsey knocked Tunney to the canvas floor in the 7th round. Instead of going to a neutral corner as he should have, Dempsey stood over the fallen Tunney, wanting to hit him again as soon as Tunney tried to get up. The referee moved Dempsey away, but by the time the fight resumed Tunney had been down for 14 to 15 seconds, instead of the 10 seconds necessary for a knockout. This became known as the famous "long count." As it turned out, Tunney again won a 10-round decision from the judges.

During the 1930s, another great black champion, Joe Louis (1914–81), made boxing history. He came from a poor farm family in Alabama but learned to box in Detroit, where he used the money his mother gave him for violin lessons to take secret boxing lessons. He dropped his last name (Barrow) when he began fighting so his mother would not know, but she forgave him when he brought home his first purse of $59. It was 1934, the time of the Great Depression, and jobs were scarce. Louis avoided the difficulties of Jack Johnson, rose quickly through the boxing ranks, but lost to the German champion Max Schmeling in 1936. In 1937, nonetheless, Louis won the world title from James Braddock. In 1938, in a return bout, Louis

knocked out Schmeling in a little more than two minutes of the first round. In that time Louis threw 50 punches and Schmeling only 2. To many in the United States, Louis's victory was seen as a symbolic triumph over the Nazi philosophy of Germany's ruler Adolf Hitler, even though Schmeling was not a Nazi.

Louis retired as undefeated champion in 1949, but ran out of money. In addition, he owed the United States government about $1 million in taxes. The Brown Bomber, as he was called, tried a comeback, lost to Ezzard Charles (1950) and Rocky Marciano (1951), and retired again in 1951. Congress eventually passed a law to forgive the debt and later honored Louis with burial in Arlington National Cemetery. In spite of a quiet manner, Louis left a sports comment embedded in our language. During preparation for a 1941 fight, his opponent, Billy Conn, who was 40 pounds lighter, said that he would merely run backward and avoid Louis's deliberate shuffling pace. In response, Louis muttered, "He can run, but he can't hide." Louis caught and clobbered him in the 13th round.

At a time when America was still strongly segregated, Louis's career was a point of pride for black Americans. Reverend Jesse

Muhammad Ali: "Float like a butterfly, Sting like a bee"

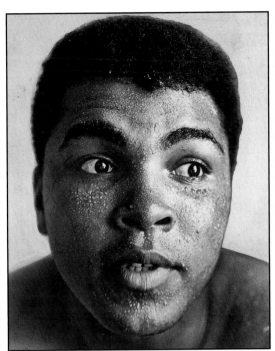

A perspiring Cassius Clay (Mohammed Ali) finishes a drill session in 1965.

He had enormous talent as a boxer and an engaging means of self-promotion. Before his championship challenge fight with Sonny Liston in 1964, the so-called Louisville Lip announced, "I'm the greatest!" That turned out to be true, as Liston found out. As the champion fell, the fans chanted Clay's fighting motto, "Float like a butterfly, sting like a bee." This phrase characterized his ring style of dancing around his opponents and hitting them with lightning punches.

Cassius Clay was born in Louisville, Kentucky, in 1942 and started fighting amateur bouts at age 12. He won the light-heavyweight division in the 1960 Olympics and turned to professional fighting. After defeating Liston, Clay announced his membership in the Nation of Islam, often called the Black Muslims, and changed his name to Muhammad Ali.

In 1967 Ali courageously refused induction into the army, and possible service in Vietnam, on the basis of religion. As historian David K. Wiggins wrote, "A large portion of the country's white community and a smaller segment of the black population were appalled by Ali's actions." Trial, conviction, and appeal took Ali away from fighting for three years during the prime of his youth, but the conviction was set aside in 1971. Ali resumed his career in 1970 when the city of Atlanta granted him a license to fight.

In 1971, Ali lost to "Smokin'" Joe Frazier in a savage fight in Madison Square Garden in New York City. This happened in spite of his prediction, "I'm gonna come out smokin' and I won't be jokin'. I'm gonna be a peckin' and a pokin', pouring water on his smokin'. It might shock you and amaze ya, but I'm gonna destroy Joe Fraziah!" In 1974 he beat George Foreman in Kinshasa, Zaire—the first heavyweight championship held in Africa— which Ali called the "rumble in the jungle." He used a "rope-a-dope" technique whereby he leaned against the ropes and protected his face with his gloves. Foreman wore himself out trying to pound Ali with body punches. Ali knocked Foreman out in the 8th round and regained the title of heavyweight champion. In 1975 Ali beat Joe Frazier in a rematch in the Philippines, a hard fight that Ali labeled "the thrilla in Manila."

Ali lost his title and regained it in 1978. He retired and then failed in a comeback fight in 1980. He retired permanently and now suffers from Parkinson's syndrome, presumedly due to the brain damage accrued during his fighting career. Because of satellite television, fighting talent, and his flamboyant personality, Ali became internationally famous. He was a source of black pride, and following the end of the Vietnam War, which many people came to regard as a mistake, Ali became a national hero for his stand against the war.

Jackson, a black leader of the 1980s and 1990s, listened to Louis's fights on the radio when he was a boy. Jackson said that it was an inspiration to hear at the end of the match, ". . . and still heavyweight champion of the world, Joe Louis."

There were other fine fighters in the 20th century, such as Sugar Ray Robinson, but certainly the most interesting was Muhammad Ali. Born in Louisville in 1942, he won an Olympic gold medal in 1960, and then the heavyweight championship from Sonny Liston in 1964. Following this victory he announced that he was changing his name from Cassius Clay to Muhammad Ali, and that he was a member of the controversial Nation of Islam, or Black Muslims. After being drafted in 1967, a time of growing debate about the U.S. involvement in the Vietnam War, he refused induction into the army. "I ain't got no quarrels with them Viet Congs," he said. Ali was sentenced to five years in prison, stripped of his championship, and was forbidden to fight. Although he never went to jail, no state would grant him a license to box. In 1971, the U.S. Supreme Court set aside his sentence. Ali then went on to fight a series of epic bouts against George Foreman, Joe Frazier, Leon Spinks, and others before he retired in 1981. He was the only fighter to win the heavyweight championship three separate times.

Prizefighting, the old sport of the fancy, thus flourished in the 19th and 20th centuries, although it never escaped its history.

Blood, violence, and gambling remained. Another sport of long interest was horse racing, and it also prospered as it galloped into the modern period. After the "Race of the Century" in 1823, local racetracks and horse racing organizations sprang up across the continent. The oldest existing race, the Queen's Plate, started in 1860 at the Toronto Turf Club with the intent of encouraging horse breeding in Canada.

During the Civil War, Southerners sold their racehorses to the Confederacy, which provided the South with a clearly superior cavalry. New courses opened after the war, the most famous being Churchill Downs in Louisville in 1875. In this last quarter of the 19th century, shorter races replaced four-mile heats, which allowed more races per day. This placed emphasis on the speed of the horse rather than stamina, and increased the opportunity to gamble. Stakes races, whereby the horse owners paid an entry fee that became part of the prize for the winner, started with the Belmont in Westchester County, New York, in 1867, Preakness in Baltimore in 1873, and the Kentucky Derby at Louisville in 1875. These events became the Triple Crown of horse racing.

Early in the 20th century a religious campaign against gambling slowed horse racing until the Great Depression of the 1930s. Then, with states desperately looking for money, pari-mutuel betting was approved in many locations. With such wagers, the winning gamblers divide the total amount of money bet on a particular race, minus a fee reserved for the racecourse. The significant Triple Crown winners of the 1930s and 1940s were Gallant Fox, War Admiral, Whirlaway, and Assault. The most famous recent Triple Crown winner, however, was the amazing Secretariat (1970–89) in 1973. In the Kentucky Derby, the big red horse flying the blue and white silks of Meadow Stables came from last place to win in record time. At the Preakness, he was six horse lengths behind when his jockey let him run, and he won by two lengths. At the Belmont, Secretariat opened an astonishing lead of 31 lengths and shattered the world record by galloping the mile-and-a-half race in 2 minutes 24 seconds.

Horse racing inspired what are likely the earliest sports songs—Stephen Foster's "Camptown Races" (1850), and probably "The Old Grey Mare," adapted from the tune "Down in Alabam'," written by J. Warner in 1858. Lady Suffolk (1833–53), the first harness horse to break 2 minutes 30 seconds in a one-mile race, was known as "The Old Grey Mare." She pulled a butcher cart until she began a belated racing career when five years old. The grey mare was a horse for hire from a livery on Long Island when her pacing abilities became apparent. David Bryan, her owner, entered Lady Suffolk in a race and won $11. She then continued to race 161 more times and won her owner about $60,000.

In a trot gait, the right front and left rear feet move at the same time, which minimizes swaying when the horse pulls a cart. As American roads improved, trotting horses became prized, and in 1813 the first harness racing track was built next to Harlem's Red House Tavern. Pacing horses from Canada, which moved both legs on a side forward at the same time, entered harness racing in the last part of the 19th century. At this time the drivers began to race with a sulky, a light-weight, one-person, two-wheeled carriage. Harness racing became popular first at county and state fairs, but after World War II it moved to the large city tracks. Along with horse racing, it had to fight competition in gambling from state lotteries and declining attendance at meets.

Although controlled by state commissions, horse racing like boxing retained a certain shadow from its background as a gambling sport of the fancy. Bowling, however, escaped its history. With larger pins to increase scoring, bowling boomed after the Civil War and began moving out of the saloons into special halls. The American Bowling Congress formed in 1895 and encouraged women to join with the men in playing the game. The Women's National Bowling Association started in 1916, which became the Women's International Bowling Congress in 1971.

The increase in the number of bowling alleys, teams, and clubs was steady through the 20th century, except for a pause during

the Great Depression, when the economy slowed down. The Professional Bowlers Association began a tour in 1958, and in 1975 Earl Anthony became the first player to earn more than $100,000 in a season. Comparable development for women did not follow, however, because of the lack of television sponsorship for women. Bowling, nonetheless, divorced itself from its saloon partnership, moved to the suburbs after World War II, and became a respectable working-class family activity.

With the growing interest in sports in the new industrial society came a question about who should participate in them. It was all right for some lower-class people to become professional boxers, for example,

Secretariat won the Kentucky Derby, Preakness, and Belmont Stakes to capture the Triple Crown in 1973.

The American Bowling Congress, formed in 1895, encouraged women to play with men. A few women spectators can be identified by their hats in the front row, right, at this 1905 Milwaukee tournament.

but not for elites, who might endanger life and limb. Generally, managers of factory workers felt that sports might detract from work, or worse, injure the laborers so that they could not work. Thus businessmen discouraged participation, even if the workers were eager. Yet, for the training of middle-class or upper-class boys, so it was thought, sports offered an important means of developing proper character. Charles Kingsley (1819–75), an Anglican clergyman in England, gave the classic moral argument:

> Through sport boys acquire virtues which no books can give them; not merely daring and endurance, but, better still, temper, self-restraint, fairness, honour, unenvious approbation of another's success, and all that 'give and take' of life which stand a man in good stead when he goes forth into the world, and without which, indeed, his success is always maimed and partial.

Especially important in England was the concept of fair play. This meant more than just playing by the rules and winning. It meant participating with ease and poise; losing with dignity; and never cheating or taking an unequal opportunity. The Corinthian Casuals, which brought together England's best soccer players for international play in the 1880s, would expose their goal when a penalty kick was assessed against them. They believed that it was wrong to foul even if it was accidental. Ideas about fair play and participation penetrated the English school system. An 1889 cartoon in the British magazine *Punch* portrayed a headmaster scolding a new student: "Of course you needn't *work* Fitzmilksoppe: but *play* you must and shall."

A similar notion was embodied in the idea that athletes should play out of love of athletics, not for the hope of making money. *Amateur* was a French word meaning "lover" and was first used in regard to gentlemen who watched boxing matches in England. It came to mean a person who participated for the love of a sport and received no money for the activity. Working-class people had difficulty with this attitude because they needed to earn money in order to survive. Only wealthy people could afford the time to practice sports and participate without financial reward. Thus the amateur ideal created a class discrimination that banned working people from sports.

The line between amateurs and professionals, those who made money from a sport, was drawn by the British schools and clubs, and adopted in America. Founded by 14 track and field enthusiasts in 1868 at the Elysian Fields, the New York Athletic Club defined an amateur as "any person who has never competed in an open competition for public or admission money, or with professionals for a prize . . . nor has at any period in his life taught or assisted in the pursuit of athletic exercises as a means of livelihood." The club established the first national championships in track and field in 1876; swimming in 1877; and boxing, fencing, and wrestling in 1878. The definition was used in those sports and adopted by the National Association of Amateur Athletes of America (N4A) in 1879. That initial national governing body dissolved in 10 years and was replaced by the Amateur Athletic Union (AAU) in 1888, which carried on the same ideal. By 1898 the AAU ruled over 250,000 athletes.

Enforcement of the amateur code was never completely successful, and its history is marked with a great deal of grief. In England, for example, a split in rugby started in 1894 when manual workers were not allowed "broken-time payments," money given by a club to replace lost wages that resulted from practice and travel to matches. In America, the great Jim Thorpe had to return the medals he had earned at the 1912 Olympic games in Stockholm, Sweden, after it was learned he had earned money as a semiprofessional baseball player. There was continual trouble about "shamateurism," efforts to pay amateurs, a problem partially resolved by the passage of the 1978 Amateur Sports Act, which allowed payment to athletes for training purposes. Echoes of the amateur ideal can be heard still in the 1990s with regard to "illegal" payments to college athletes.

After World War II, bowling was a respectable working-class activity. Here, a mother brings along her infant when she goes to the bowling alley in 1963.

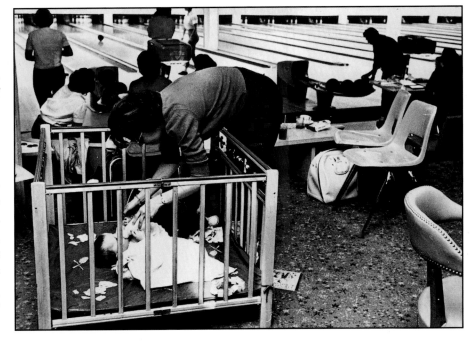

Chapter 5

Participants and Sports

Cyclists cross the Mirabeau Bridge over the Durance River during the 1951 Tour de France. The race covers about 3,000 miles over 25 days. Armand Baeyens of Belgium won this particular stage of the race, about 130 miles, in a time of 7:15:41.

ontinuing industrialization and urbanization in the United States and Canada made possible greater leisure for all people. Other sports beyond the interest of the fancy made their way into American culture. The public not only became sports spectators, but also participants in sporting activity. Seemingly, a person who participated in a sport for recreation would have some understanding of the competitive aspects of the activity as well. In the late 20th century such dual activities applied to many sports, including swimming, bicycling, bowling, golf, jogging, volleyball, and tennis.

Changing transportation technology provided opportunities to ride and race bicycles. Ernest Michaux of France put a crank and pedals on the front wheel of a bicycle in 1855. This was followed by various improvements. The iron-framed bicycle of the English firm, Reynolds and May, in 1869 featured huge front and small back wheels; the 1887 J. K. Starley "safety bike" from England, which was similar to modern bicycles, had a diamond-shaped frame, sprocket, chain reaching to the rear tire, and brakes; and pneumatic, rubber

tires developed by John Dunlop of Belfast, Ireland, in 1890 made riding more comfortable. Measured in terms of energy used to travel a distance, these rapid technical changes made the bicycle the most efficient means of transport ever invented.

Bicycle clubs in Europe and the United States, formed for social outings, lobbied local governments for smoother roads. Women found a way to move about town on their own and wore new-fashioned, loose trousers gathered at the ankles and called "bloomers." It was a step in the march for increased freedom for women. "Daisy," a popular song about a proposal of marriage and riding a bicycle built for two, was written in 1892 by Harry Dacre. Cycling, like several other activities of the late 19th century, thus included an important element of social participation. By 1896 there were 1 million bicycles in use in North America.

Racing came quickly for bicycles—the first competition on wheels without horses. In 1891 the Bordeaux-to-Paris race began. The International Cyclists Association formed and held a world championship in Chicago in 1893, and six-day races in New

FOR HEALTH & RECREATION

RIDE A CRAWFORD BICYCLE

$60 NONE BETTER
FEW AS GOOD $75

This 1896 poster advertises health and recreation—and socializing—via bicycling. Though the woman pictured wears a dress, bicycling brought a certain amount of freedom to women, who were permitted to wear bloomers while riding.

York's Madison Square Garden started in 1895. Velodromes, with their steeply banked oval tracks, sprouted across America, and for three decades professional riders were the most highly paid athletes in the nation. Frank Kramer, the U.S. world champion, made $20,000 in 1911 and about $500,000 during 22 years of racing. The most famous bicycle race, the Tour de France, began in 1903 as a three-week event that covered 2,500 to 3,000 miles through the mountains and countryside of six countries. It is considered the hardest of modern athletic competitions and has been dominated by Europeans. Only in 1986, 1989, and 1990 was an American, Greg LeMond, counted among the winners.

Bicycle racing, however, declined in popularity as increasing numbers of people gave up their bikes for automobiles. It was a bad sign when Albert Pope, the so-called father of U.S. cycling, appeared at the bicycle exhibition in Madison Square Garden in 1899 driving a new electric runabout car. Automobile racing arose with the evolution of the car, and Henry Ford built the first racer, the 80-horsepower "999." He hired Barney Oldfield, a bicycle racer who had never driven a car, to race the machine. Oldfield set a world record of 91.37 miles per hour with the car in 1904. Ford thought that racing was good business for his automobile company and said it provided "advertising of the only kind that people care to read."

The Automobile Club of America, later the American Automobile Association (AAA), sponsored a Thanksgiving Day race in Savannah in 1908 that attracted a crowd of 200,000 fans. In 1909 the two-and-a-

Ray Harroun, winner of the first Memorial Day race at the Indianapolis Motor Speedway in 1911.

half-mile oval track of the Indianapolis Motor Speedway opened; in 1911 it was paved with brick. The first Memorial Day 500-mile race was held that year at the newly paved "brickyard." It was won by Ray Harroun with an average speed of 74.59 miles per hour. The first cars carried the driver and a mechanic, but in the 1930s sleek, low-slung, single-seat cars began averaging more than 100 miles per hour. In 1961 Jack Brabham from Australia drove a rear-engine Cooper-Climax car to ninth place and started a shift to vehicles with the engine in back. Jacques Villeneuve of Canada won the 1995 race with an average speed of 153.6 miles per hour. A split between organizers in 1996 created two groups of racers, the Indy Racing League (IRL) and the Championship Auto Racing Teams (CART). Stock car competition under the direction of the National Association for Stock Car Auto Racing (NASCAR) was organized in 1947. High spectator attendance at the various races confirm a lasting fascination with the automobile.

Tennis, golf, swimming, volleyball, and skiing also developed a dual spectator and participant following in the 20th century. In 1874 Major Walter Clopton Wingfield patented a game of tennis in England. For $26 he sold a package that included a net, racquets, balls, and a set of rules. His court was in the shape of an hour-glass, narrow at the net. The net was almost five feet high and scoring was similar to badminton. The All England Croquet and Lawn Tennis Club rewrote the rules in 1877 to lower the net to 3 feet 3 inches at the center and make the court rectangular. Meanwhile, in 1874 Mary Ewing Outerbridge from Staten Is-

land, New York, saw the game played by British officers in Bermuda. This was a game that could be played by women. She bought equipment and soon tennis was being played at the Staten Island Cricket and Base Ball Club. That same year tennis was played in Nahant, Massachusetts, and Toronto. By the end of the decade, James Gordon Bennett had his tiff with the Reading Room and built the Newport Casino. Formed from 19 clubs in 1881, the United States Lawn Tennis Association (called the United States Tennis Association after 1975) held its first championship that same year at the Casino.

The sport spread rapidly through upper-class country clubs and schools. In 1899 a group of Harvard players played demon-

First played on close-cropped grass, lawn tennis was soon played on asphalt and concrete surfaces, and the word "lawn" was dropped.

"Big Bill" Tilden (far left), American tennis star of the 1920s and 1930s, was chiefly responsible for U.S. retention of the Davis Cup until 1926.

Cartoonist Sam Wells depicts former tennis champion Norman Brooks exhorting his fellow Australians Frank Sedgman, Bill Sidwell, and John Bromwich to win the 1949 Davis Cup.

stration matches on the West Coast, including British Columbia. One of the players, Dwight F. Davis, donated a trophy to encourage international play. England accepted the challenge, but lost the match in 1900 to the United States team in the first Davis Cup tournament. After 1903 the competition expanded beyond the United States and Great Britain, and was dominated by Australian and American players.

In sunny California, meanwhile, where good weather made possible a long season, tennis enthusiasts inspired by the Harvard tour built concrete and asphalt public courts. To the surprise of the easterners in 1909, red-haired Maurice McLoughlin (1890–1957), the "California Comet," suddenly appeared. Having grown up on the California hard-surface courts, McLoughlin presented a new style of play that featured a booming serve, rushing the net, and long, hard ground strokes. By the time he won a national title in 1912, the first for anyone beyond the Mississippi River, McLoughlin had changed tennis.

During the 1920s, tall, dramatic "Big Bill" Tilden dominated men's tennis—the first American to win a singles champion-

ship at England's Wimbledon tournament in 1920—while Helen Wills of the United States and Suzanne Lenglen of France became the first well-known women athletes through tennis. Neither Tilden nor Lenglen was able to establish professional tennis on a permanent basis, but in 1968 the All England Club opened its prestigious Wimbledon tournament to both professionals and amateurs. John A. "Jack" Kramer from Las Vegas, who was a tennis star of the 1940s, organized a professional Grand Prix tour, which with the help of television money became successful.

Women were left out, but Billie Jean King, with the aid of Gladys Heldman, publisher of *World Tennis* magazine, put together the Women's International Tennis Association and their own tour sponsored by the Philip Morris Corporation in 1970–71. The women's professional effort was successful, and in 1971 King became the first woman athlete to win more than $100,000 in prize money. "Money is what people respect," King said, "and when you are a professional athlete, they want to know how much you have made. They judge you on that." This development of

open tennis and equal pay for women made possible the later accomplishments of Martina Navratilova, Chris Evert, Boris Becker, Jimmy Connors, John McEnroe, and others.

Meanwhile, the equipment improved, particularly the racket. The frame was made of wood until the 1960s, and when unused the racket had to be kept in a frame to prevent warping. Manufacturers began to use steel frames in 1967, aluminum in 1968, and fiberglass with graphite in the 1970s. The Wilson company introduced the steel T2000 in 1967 based on a 40-year-old design by Rene Lacoste (who also produced tennis ball practice machines and sport shirts). The T2000 had a round head, open frame that reduced drag, and strings attached to metal clips. The strings flexed on impact with the ball, and sent it back with sling-shot power. The T2000 was the vanguard of the technical revolution in tennis. Prince Manufacturing introduced a racket, invented by Howard Head, with twice as much hitting surface, in 1976. In the late 1980s, "widebody" rackets with thicker frames made of Kevlar composites became available. The result

Billie Jean King: The Battle of the Sexes

She began playing tennis at age 11, was 4 times the U.S. Open singles champion, and won a record 20 times at Wimbledon in the 1960s and 1970s. Born in Long Beach, California, in 1943 to a working-class family, she chose to pursue a tennis career at a time when American women were expected to become homemakers and raise children. Her maturity as a tennis star came at the same time as a movement for greater freedom for women in the United States. She explained how she became involved:

When it comes to Women's Lib, I'm pretty much of a pragmatist, and I'd bet that most other women are too. Maybe you start comparing paychecks and find you're not making as much as the guy sitting next to you who's doing the same work. Or you apply to med school and find out you're going to be the only woman in a class of 200. Or you want to keep in shape when you're in college and learn there isn't any women's intramural sports program, but that the university has just contracted for a $3.5 million basketball arena. Little things like that. Pretty soon you start thinking. . . . Then you decide to do something about it and all of a sudden you're part of the Movement. That's pretty much what happened with me.

In 1970 King and other top women boycotted a tournament that offered $12,500 to the male winner and only $1,500 to the female. With Gladys Heldman, publisher of *World Tennis*, she organized the Virginia Slims Tournament for women. When the U.S. Lawn Tennis Association (USLTA) suspended her along with the other competing women, King formed the Women's Tennis Association (WTA). In 1973 the USLTA and WTA agreed that awards at the U.S. Open tournament would be equal for men and women. King said about her battle, "Almost every day for the last four years someone comes up to me and says, 'Hey, when are you going to have children?' I say, 'I'm not ready yet.' They say, 'Why aren't you at home?' I say, 'Why don't you go ask Rod Laver [a male professional tennis star] why he isn't at home?'"

King used her prize money to establish *WomenSports* magazine (after 1985, *Women's Sports and Fitness*) and the Women's Sports Foundation in 1974 to encourage female athletics. But she did something more. King dramatically demonstrated feminine athletic ability at the so-called Battle of the Sexes in the Houston Astrodome in 1973. Bobby Riggs (1918–95), who had been Wimbledon champion in 1939, challenged and beat Margaret Court, a leading player from Australia, on Mother's Day in 1973. Riggs was a self-described "hustler" who made money from tennis games and was taking advantage of the women's movement. He next challenged King and they met in Houston on September 30, 1973. Riggs promised that he would "set women's lib back twenty years, to get women back in the home, where they belong."

Both used "hype" in the match—King was brought to the court on a litter carried by handsome men; Riggs accompanied by beautiful women. King won easily, 6-4, 6-3, 6-3. Afterward, they cordially congratulated each other in front of 30,000 spectators and a huge television audience, the largest number ever to watch a tennis match. King with her aggressive, bounding style had shown that women could be excellent athletes and were worth watching. Interestingly, the two players remained friends, and King wrote a touching obituary about Riggs for *Sports Illustrated* in 1995. He admitted to her that he did not know the first thing about the movement for women's liberation.

Billie Jean King smashes a return at her opponent Carol Caldwell during the third round singles match at Wimbeldon in 1962. King ousted top-seeded Margaret Smith to win the women's singles title.

was that players could hit harder with less effort. The technology made the two-handed backhand stroke especially effective, a shot popularized by Jimmy Connors and Chris Evert.

Golf, like tennis, was imported in the last part of the 19th century and became a staple activity for the members of country clubs. It was actually imported twice, because there is evidence of the Scottish game in colonial America. The estate of New York's governor in 1729 listed ten clubs and seven dozen balls, and Albany, New York, posted a law against playing on Sunday in 1760. More than 100 years later, the Montreal Golf Club built a course. In 1873, John Reid, who learned the game from a friend, laid out a three-hole course in a Yonkers, New York, cow pasture and organized the St. Andrews Golf Club in 1887. In 1891, millionaire William K. Vanderbilt brought Willie Dunn, a golf professional from Scot-

Wooden tennis rackets (above) were replaced, by and large, in 1967 when the revolutionary Wilson T2000 (below) was introduced. The T2000 revolutionized tennis in terms of the speed and power of play.

land, to design a nine-hole course at the opulent Shinnecock Hills Golf Club at Southampton, Long Island. In Scotland, where the courses were built along coastal "links" of land, there were natural hazards formed by the sea. In North America, the designers built artificial hazards of small lakes, trees, and sand traps as a part of the course, or links.

Five country clubs formed the Amateur Golf Association in 1894. It shortly became the U.S. Golf Association and held a championship in 1895 at Newport. By 1900 there were more than 1,000 courses in North America. The game, quite correctly, was viewed as an upper-class pastime. In a democratic nation where politicians had to appeal to common people, President Theodore Roosevelt warned his successor William Howard Taft to avoid the game. "I myself play tennis, but the game is a little more familiar," Roosevelt said. "Besides you never saw a photograph of me playing tennis. I am careful about that; photographs on horseback, yes; tennis, no. And golf is fatal." Taft ignored the advice and became the first golf-playing President of the United States in 1908.

British players on tour in the United States almost always won the matches, but in 1913 at the American Open at the Brookline, Massachusetts, Country Club, Francis Ouimet (1893–1967) scored an upset. Born in Brookline, he was the son of a French-Canadian father and Irish-American mother. The path to his grammar school led across the golf course and Ouimet became interested in the game. In 1913, to the surprise of everyone, the 20-year-old Ouimet tied the British pro-

fessionals, Ted Ray and Harry Vardon. In a playoff the next day on a rain-soaked course the amateur Ouimet beat Vardon by five strokes and Ray by seven. It made a great newspaper story about the average American boy beating the British professionals. Ouimet went on to win the U.S. amateur titles in 1914, 1920, and 1931. He was, in addition, a representative of the United States on the Walker Cup teams from 1922 to 1949. Beginning in 1922, the Walker Cup brought British and American amateur teams into competition. Ouimet's victory gave the United States a new sports hero and helped to change golf's image— no longer was it a sport just for the idle rich.

Cities began to build public courses, and golf became a status symbol for businessmen. Now the middle class could share in the recreation. The equipment also changed. The original golf ball was made of leather and stuffed with feathers. Solid balls made of gutta-percha, a rubberlike substance, became available in 1848, and rubber-core balls at the end of the century. According to golf folklore, players noticed that when hit the new balls with smooth surfaces tended to hook (the ball flies to the left of a right-handed player, or right of a left-handed player), or slice (the ball curves to the right of a right-handed player, or the left of a left-handed player). Old balls with cut-up surfaces tended to fly in a straight line. The result was that ballmakers began to put indentations, or dimples, in the balls in 1908. Club handles were made of ash or hickory wood until 1926, when tubular steel shafts began to be used. The new shafts provided greater control, accuracy, and power for the player's swing.

At the same 1913 open tournament with Ouimet, a young American professional, Walter C. Hagan (1892–1969), showed up wearing white buck shoes, white flannel pants, striped silk shirt, red bandanna, and checkered cap. He announced brashly to the defending champion, John McDermott, "I've come down here to help you fellows stop Vardon and Ray." It was Ouimet rather than Hagan who did the job, but Hagan became the most important professional player of the 1920s.

"Sir Walter," as he was nicknamed, was the first to make a living playing golf, although he said he only made $1 million and spent $2 million. He broke down the snobbery of private country clubs when he forced them to accept him in the locker rooms. He set fashion on the links by popularizing color-coordinated "plus-fours," or knickers. His colorful personality also brought to the game a great deal of publicity, such as the time after spending the night out he arrived at the first tee in a limousine. Hagan stepped out, kissed the hand of a mink-draped women in the back seat, and proceeded to play the first round in his tuxedo and patent leather shoes.

Although Hagan won the Professional Golfers' Association (PGA) tournament, which started in 1916, four times in his career, he beat Bobby Jones only once. Robert T. "Bobby" Jones, Jr. (1902–71), born to a wealthy Atlanta family, was a child prodigy and won the Atlanta Junior Championship at age nine. He had a terrible temper, which he learned to control, and won 13 major titles. He retired at age 28 in 1930 after winning the "grand slam"—the American Amateur, American Open, Brit-

Walter Hagan, the first man to make a living playing professional golf, was known as a flashy dresser on the course. Fans were attracted to his equally showy personality, and nicknamed him "Sir Walter" and "The Haig."

ish Amateur, and British Open tournaments. He was given a ticker-tape parade in New York City. Jones later said, "First come my wife and children. Next comes my profession—the law. Finally, and never as a life in itself, comes golf."

As golf's popularity grew, fans became interested in watching the good players. In 1936, when Jones appeared at St. Andrews in Scotland for a quiet round of golf, the word quickly spread. Five thousand spectators were waiting at the first tee. Stores closed, and by the 18th tee there were 7,000 fans following his game. Later champions such as Ben Hogan, Byron Nelson, and Sam Snead also attracted fans, but televised

A perfectionist given to temper tantrums, Bobby Jones eventually came to be admired for his unfailing sportsmanship. This multiple-exposure photo demonstrates Jones's perfect golf swing.

Neither Arnold Palmer, nor the crowd behind him, can believe he missed this easy putt in 1964. Palmer lost this tournament, the Thunderbird Classic, to Tony Lema.

matches in the 1960s brought the largest surge of popularity. The cameras brought the drama of each hole to the viewer. Meanwhile, "Arnie's Army" of fans flowed over the links marching after their hero, Arnold Palmer, even when he was not playing well.

Born in Youngstown, Ohio, in 1929, Palmer began learning to play when he was three years old. He was the son of the golf professional at the Latrobe, Pennsylvania, Country Club, and he became U.S. Amateur champion in 1954. In his career Palmer won the prestigious invitational Masters Tournament, which began in 1934, four times. Fans, who often played the game themselves, groaned with Palmer when he missed putts and grinned with him when a spectacular surge from behind brought victory. They could easily identify with his emotions, which were plain to see. In 1962, Palmer became the first golfer to make more than $100,000 in one season.

Even Bobby Jones, however, recognized that the greatest player of the century was Jack W. Nicklaus. Born in Columbus, Ohio, in 1940, Nicklaus was nicknamed "The Golden Bear" for early pudginess and

blond hair. He won six Masters and five PGA tournaments, mainly in the 1960s and 1970s. Nicklaus was known for long accurate drives and steady putts. His single weakness was a sand shot, but his skills kept him out of the sand most of the time. Palmer's fans hated him. His 1986 victory in the Masters may well have been his most spectacular. Well past his prime as a player at age 46, Nicklaus came from eighth place to win in the final round by a single stroke.

Television money and tournament support from business corporations added to the popularity of golf. Women who played at the country clubs during restricted hours began to compete as amateurs and professionals. The Women's Professional Golf Association, which started in 1946, was replaced with the Ladies' Professional Golf Association in 1948. Its purpose was to create a national professional tour for women. Fourteen years after Palmer, Judy Rankin became the first woman golfer to win more than $100,000 in a season. The mark of successful professionals, male or female, thus became whether or not they could win enough money on the tour to make a living.

Golf and tennis were sports imported to North America that attracted broad recreational participation. The same was true about skiing. Norwegian immigrants brought cross-country skiing to North America as a form of winter transportation in the 1850s. At the same time, workers on the mountain mining frontier of western America used skis for both transport and recreation. The Norwegian Ski Club of Minneapolis hosted a cross-country race in 1885, and the Montreal Ski Club held a ski

Jack Nicklaus tosses his cap away after sinking a crucial putt on the 18th green to win the 1963 Masters Golf Tournament by one stroke.

jumping contest in 1907. Meanwhile, enthusiasts founded the National Ski Association in 1904 to promote the sport and to hold national championships. Alpine, or downhill, racing originated in Austria during the decade after World War I. Slalom racing through spaced gates, or sets of poles, on a downhill course came from the same area, and was inspired by skiing through trees. Charles Proctor, a skiing enthusiast and physics professor from Dartmouth College, laid out the first slalom course in North America in 1925.

Ironically, hard economic times were a boost for this sport. During the Great Depression, the U.S. government paid for building ski trails—the Works Progress Administration (WPA) sponsored more than 40,000 recreation and sports facilities projects of all kinds from 1935 to 1941. The WPA spent $1 million to develop the Timberline Lodge ski area near Portland, Oregon. By 1940 there were about 2 million recreational skiers in the United States, and about 30,000 in Canada. During World War II, mountain troops learned to ski and returned with enthusiasm to the activity after the war. For example, the 10th Mountain Division trained in Colorado, and following the end of the war members of that group came back to the mountains to develop the ski industry of the state. As a result, the town of Aspen became popular as a ski resort.

Nordic skiing, cross-country skiing, and ski jumping became a part of the Olympic games in 1924. Alpine skiing was added in 1948. Alpine World Cup competition for professionals started in 1967, and generally, the ski champions have come from Eu-

rope—France, Norway, Switzerland, Germany, Austria, and Italy. Nancy Greene of Canada, however, won the World Cup in 1967 and 1968; Phil Mahre of the United States in 1981, 1982, and 1983; Tamara McKinney of the United States in 1983. Long-standing interest, winter weather, and easy access to suitable mountains explain the European success.

As with golf and tennis, technology added to skiing proficiency. To replace wood, Howard Head, who also worked on tennis rackets, developed the first laminated ski in 1946. He used aluminum, plywood, and plastic to make a "metal sandwich." He tested some 40 versions before inventing a successful one in 1950. The Head ski was three times more flexible than wooden

The U.S. ski team is ready for its international meet in Chamonix, France. The event was originally scheduled as the 1962 world championships, but several communist nations pulled out over a visa dispute.

Riding on the shoulders of her German teammates, skier Heidi Biebl smiles and waves to the crowd of spectators after beating the favored Penny Pitou of the U.S. in the ladies' downhill championships in 1960.

ones. This allowed the skier to turn much more easily than before, or as skiers say, to "carve" through the snow in the curves.

By far the most popular participant activity has been swimming. Benjamin Franklin advocated swimming in the 18th century and gave demonstrations in the Thames River of England. In the mid 19th century "sea-bathing" began to be popular at resorts in England and the United States. Large numbers of people, however, were taught to swim at the YMCAs that spread across the continent and the world in the last part of the century. Country clubs and athletic clubs also added swimming pools and taught the skill. The Dolphin Club of Toronto in 1875 and the Montreal Swim Club in 1876 were the first organizations to sponsor races. The New York Athletic Club (NYAC) held a U.S. championship in 1883.

Most competitive swimmers used breaststroke in competition until the end of the century. J. Arthur Trudgen, from England, saw South Americans using a hand-over-hand action, and he combined it with a scissors kick. This became the "Trudgen" stroke. An Englishman who had moved to Australia, Frederick Cavill, noticed South Sea natives using an overhand stroke with an up and down flutter kick in 1878. His son, Richard, returned to England in 1902 and became the first swimmer to swim 100 yards in less than one minute. Newspaper reports of the feat called it "like crawling over the water," and thus it was known as the Australian crawl. Australians called it the "splash stroke." In the United States, Charles M. Daniels of the New York Athletic Club synchronized the kick with the arm action—six kicks per cycle—and set a world record of 56 seconds for 100 yards in 1906. This was called the American crawl and became the dominant and fastest stroke for racing.

The Amateur Athletic Union (AAU) took over the national meet from the NYAC in 1888. It added breaststroke competition in 1906, backstroke in 1934, and butterfly in 1952. Water polo began to be played in England, with men riding barrels painted like horses. Without the barrels, it became

A member of the New York Athletic Club scores in a water polo contest in 1904. The NYAC was one of the leaders in water polo at the time.

an Olympic sport in 1900 and was supervised by the AAU in the United States after 1906. The New York Athletic Club and the Illinois Athletic Club dominated the sport in the United States until after World War II.

The Illinois Athletic Club also developed one of the most remarkable swimmers of the 1920s, Johnny Weissmuller (1904–84). He was a sprinter born in Chicago who set world records in every crawl event up to 880 yards. His record of 51.0 seconds for 100 yards set in 1927 was not broken until 1943. Tall, broad-chested, and handsome, Weissmuller won a total of five Olympic gold medals. His fame as a swimmer led him to Hollywood, where he starred in 19 Tarzan movies. As Tarzan, Weissmuller was famous for developing a yodeling "elephant call," swinging through the trees, and using simple language—"Me Tarzan, you Jane." Most importantly, he publicized swimming as a sport.

Also significant for the development of swimming were several long-distance endurance performances. The most famous were the efforts to swim the icy English Channel. It was 20 miles across as a crow might fly, but with various currents it was 38 miles as a tuna might swim. In 1875, using the breaststroke, Matthew Webb of England became the first to cross the channel; his time was 21 hours 45 minutes. Others soon followed, and in 1926 Gertrude Ederle of the United States, with a time of 14 hours 23 minutes, beat the men's record

by two hours. She was given a ticker-tape parade on her return to New York City and spent the next two years traveling throughout North America and Europe giving swimming demonstrations in a collapsible swimming tank.

The publicity given to swimming by Ederle and Weissmuller, along with the ongoing programs to teach swimming in the YMCAs and other clubs, made swimming the most widespread recreational

Johnny Weissmuller, Olympic swimmer and movie star, kept his Olympic medals in a brown paper bag. He displayed the swimming medals won in the U.S. in a locked cabinet.

Gertrude Ederle: The Grease-Smeared Venus

Gertrude Ederle, shown here at a baseball practice in 1928. Known for her swimming, Ederle participated in several other activities to keep fit for water sports.

This ticker-tape parade was waiting for "Trudy" Ederle upon her triumphant return to New York City.

Born in New York City in 1906 to working-class, German-American parents, Ederle became AAU champion in distance swimming events in 1923 and 1924. She won a gold and bronze medal in the 1924 Olympics, but what attracted public attention was her 1926 swim across the English Channel in 14 hours 23 minutes. Not only was she the first woman to complete the distance, but also she had beaten the men's time by more than two hours. It was sensational. Because she had kept her body warm in the cold water by putting grease on her skin, the newspapers called her a "Grease-Smeared Venus," and "America's Best Girl." She was given a hero's welcome home to New York City and even a song was composed about her: "You're such a cutie, you're just as sweet as tutti-frutti. Trudy, who'll be the lucky fellow?"

She toured the nation and Europe giving swimming exhibitions in a portable swimming tank. Dressed in a revealing tank suit cut high across the leg, Edele helped to liberate women from the cumbersome swimming costumes that threatened them with drowning. All was not well, however. Her ears damaged by the icy water of the English Channel, she went deaf. In 1928, moreover, her busy schedule of appearances led to a "nervous breakdown." After recovering, Ederle lived a quiet life teaching deaf children how to swim.

activity. Except at the Olympic games, however, swimming lacked the appeal to become a major spectator sport in North America. For good swimmers, therefore, there was little chance for professional activity except as coaches, lifeguards, and swimming pool managers.

Like swimming, volleyball lacks spectator appeal except as an Olympic event, although beach volleyball from California has recently gained popularity through television. The game's origin is similar to that of basketball (discussed later). In 1895, William G. Morgan, who was director of the YMCA at Holyoke, Massachusetts, invented another indoor sport. Inspired by badminton, it was designed for older men who did not care to run up and down a court. The basic idea was to hit a light-

weight ball over a net, and when it was demonstrated at a conference of YMCA directors the name *volleyball* was suggested. Like basketball, it spread through the YMCA network and found a home in China, Japan, and Korea. An International Volleyball Federation began in 1947, and volleyball became an Olympic sport in 1964. It also found a place during the 1980s in American colleges, particularly as a women's sport.

There are other important participatory sports, such as softball, youth sports, school varsity sports, and the intramural activities in schools. These are closely related to those sports that can attract a television audience and large numbers of spectators. This participation, not included in this chapter, is a part of the development of the great spectator sports.

The YMCA and YWCA were instrumental in spreading certain sports such as volleyball throughout the world. This logo belongs to the YMCA.

These volleyball players wait for the decision of the referee (on ladder at left) at a YWCA camp in Payette Lakes, Idaho, around 1915.

These young sports enthusiasts enjoy a Tigers baseball game at Briggs Stadium in Detroit, Michigan, August 1942.

Chapter 6

The Great Spectator Sports of North America

Although cricket had been a part of colonial America, the sport failed to capture the interest of the people. Cricket was a sport of the English aristocracy and lingered in the Dominion of Canada. Cricket endured in other English colonies; why not in the United States? One common answer given by historians is that Americans wished to be considered separate from the old world. This meant independence not only in politics, but in cultural matters as well. It explains, supposedly, why North Americans developed football, baseball, basketball, and ice hockey apart from Europe. The answer is not quite that simple, however, because American sports have historical links to the games and sports of many groups, including Native Americans. The desire to be considered independent and different, nonetheless, gave birth to the most entrenched myth in American sports history.

When Albert G. Spalding, a former player and team owner, became the foremost manufacturer of sports equipment in the United States, he deliberately set out to prove that baseball did not come from British origins. His investigative commis-sion of 1905–7 determined that the faltering memory of an aged Denver mining engineer who wrote them a letter was correct. Baseball was invented by Abner Doubleday, who later became a Union general in the Civil War, at Cooperstown, New York, in 1839. Spalding published this opinion in his *Official Baseball Guide* of 1908. Baseball was a game "too lively for any but Americans to play," he said. Non-sense, of course, but the untruth was printed and people have believed it ever since.

Regardless of what Spalding had to say about Doubleday, American baseball origi-nated from various British bat and ball games such as stoolball, rounders, and town ball. Stoolball involved rural English milk-maids who tried to knock over a milk stool with a ball while another defended the stool with a stick; rounders used posts for bases and a batter had to run and touch the posts after a hit; town ball used stakes for bases and the batter stood between home and first base. Ideas from rounders and town ball were brought together by Alexander J. Cartwright (1820–92), a 25-year-old bank teller in New York City. He organized the Knickerbocker Base Ball Club, drew up a

Harper's Weekly *magazine published this drawing of an 1859 baseball match at the Elysian Fields in Hoboken, New Jersey.*

set of rules, and played the first baseball game at James Cox Stevens's Elysian Fields at Hoboken in 1845.

Cartwright used a diamond-shape infield with four bases placed 90 feet apart. The pitcher stood in the middle, 45 feet away, and pitched underhanded to a batter at home plate who could ask for high or low pitches. There were no called strikes, and the batter waited for a desired pitch. Each nine-person side was allowed three outs, which could be accomplished by catching the ball on the fly or first bounce, throwing to first base ahead of the runner, or tagging a runner between bases. The infielders stood on top of the bases, except for the catcher and shortstop. No one used gloves—it was considered unmanly. The umpire sat at a table near third base to keep score and settle disputes. No cursing or ungentlemanly behavior was allowed, and the game ended when a team scored 21 runs.

Initially, baseball was a social event for middle-class gentlemen, who played ball

The National Association of Base Ball Players included the Brooklyn Atlantics (top row) and the Philadelphia Athletics (bottom row). This engraving of the two teams appeared in Harper's Weekly *in 1866; the NABBP excluded black players the following year.*

wearing blue wool pants, white flannel shirts, and straw hats. The Knickerbockers usually had a dinner after the game and spectators came only by invitation. As other teams formed and began to play one another, the "New York game" quickly spread. Cartwright himself moved to Hawaii in 1849 and laid out a diamond to teach baseball to the islanders in 1852. Within a decade, the sport had become popular with the working classes in the United States, and in 1857 22 clubs formed the National Association of Base Ball Players (NABBP), which took charge of changing the rules. The organization officially excluded black players in 1867.

The Civil War helped to spread the game throughout the nation, as bored soldiers sought entertainment in the lull between battles. Southern prisoners of war learned the game and northern troops occupying the South during Reconstruction introduced baseball to local boys. With the completion of the first transcontinental railroad in 1869, the first professional team, the Cincinnati Red Stockings, traveled to California to demonstrate their prowess.

In 1873 Horace Wilson, an American teacher at Tokyo University, demonstrated baseball to his students. Hiroshi Hiraoka, a Japanese engineer who had studied in Boston and become a Red Sox fan, established the first Japanese team in 1878. Americans at the Yokohama Athletic Club in Japan arrogantly resisted a challenge from the Ichiko prep school for five years. No one could play as well Americans, so they

Late 19th-century Americans were scornful of Japanese baseball teams—until the Japanese began beating them at their own game. These two catchers, J. Nagano (left) and J. Kuji, are members of the team from Wasada University in Japan.

thought. In 1896, expecting an easy rout, the Americans finally accepted a game. They were persuaded by an English teacher at Ichiko. When asked if the field was ready for play because of bad weather, the Americans sent a telegram, "Are you trying to flee from us?"

After a bumbling start, the Japanese boys won 29-4 and, with a celebration of cheers and cups of sake, a rice wine, became national heroes. It was exhilarating to beat the Americans at their own game, and humiliating for the Americans of the Yokohama team. The American jeering stopped; it was hard to admit that foreigners might play the American pastime better than Americans. For the Japanese it was a sign that Japan was just as modern as the United States. Return games resulted in two more Japanese victories with scores of 32-9 and 22-6. Finally, when the USS *Olympia,* a battleship, steamed into port, the bedraggled Americans received enough reinforcements to win a game on July 4, 1896, by a close score of 14-12.

New teams formed in Japan, and after the Waseda School lost to a touring squad from the University of Chicago, Suishu Tobita, a student, vowed revenge. Some years after graduation he returned as a coach and stated, "If the players do not try so hard as to vomit blood in practice then they can not hope to win games. One must suffer to be good." In 1925 his team defeated the University of Chicago three times in a four-game series. Baseball in Japan was abandoned during World War II, but revived with youth teams and a two-league professional system in 1950. Baseball became Japan's most popular sport in the last half of the 20th century, and several Japanese players have moved to the American major leagues—notably, pitcher Hideo Nomo, who began playing with the Los Angeles Dodgers in 1995.

Baseball also spread to the Caribbean, especially to Cuba, Mexico, Venezuela, the Dominican Republic, and Puerto Rico. Upper-class Cuban boys sent to study in the United States returned to the island with the game in the 1860s. Leagues formed during the 1870s, and the Philadelphia Athletics toured Cuba in 1887. Baseball became the sport of the rebels who opposed Spanish rule. The Spanish, who tried to suppress the game in favor of bullfighting, lost the Spanish-American War and baseball emerged triumphant. A two-way interchange of players developed between Cuba and the United States in the early 20th century, with white and black Americans playing "winter ball" on the island with the Cubans. Outfielder Roberto Clemente of Puerto Rico, pitcher Juan Marichal of the Dominican Republic, and shortstop Luis Aparicio of Venezuela have

Roberto Clemente, a native of Puerto Rico, played his entire major-league career with the Pittsburgh Pirates. A Baseball Hall of Fame inductee, Clemente died in a plane crash while attempting to take food and medicine to earthquake victims in Nicaragua in 1972.

Amateur softball player Linda McConkey dives into third base during a 1955 exhibition game between her Lorelei Ladies and the Tomboys in Atlanta, Georgia. In the air to make the catch is Jerrie Rainey of the Tomboys. Softball remains a sport for nonprofessionals, and is a popular varsity sport for women in college.

been elected to the Baseball Hall of Fame in Cooperstown, New York.

Baseball did not spread as far as cricket or soccer, probably due to the later rise of American power compared to that of the British. The American game, however, possessed an attraction for North America and Japan. Compared to cricket as a bat and ball game, baseball games took much less time, and became a "people's game" in which working-class people could excel. It appealed to democratic, egalitarian notions in the United States. The game, moreover, was filled with heroes, villains, dramatic moments, and comedy.

Baseball's first great star was Michael J. "King" Kelly (1857–94), who played mainly for the Chicago White Sox and the Boston Nationals in his career. He was noted for his

hook and headfirst slides into bases, strong batting (.308 lifetime average), hard drinking, and on-field antics. At dusk with no lights, for instance, in a game against Boston, Kelly leaped high to grab a hit to right field. He shouted with success and headed toward the locker room. The umpire called three outs and the game ended because of darkness. In the locker room Kelly was asked where the ball was and he retorted, "How the hell would I know? It went a mile over me head!"

On another occasion, when Kelly was sitting on the bench not playing and nursing a terrific headache from too much drinking, a St. Louis player hit a foul ball his way. Kelly wanted the game to end. He stood and announced, "Kelly now catching for Chicago," and fielded the ball. This made

the final out, Chicago won, and St. Louis was outraged. There was no rule to prevent Kelly's action, but after that there could be no substitutions while the ball was in play.

Other changes refined baseball: overhand pitching started in 1884; batters lost their privilege of ordering high or low pitches in 1887; the batter was limited to three strikes in 1888; a base was awarded after four balls, pitches outside the designated area, in 1889; the present pitching distance of 60 feet 6 inches was set in 1893 (it was supposed to be 60 feet, but the surveyor misread the numbers); in the 1880s infield players moved away from the bases instead of standing on them; in the 1890s players began to use gloves; foul ball hits began to be counted as strikes in 1901; spitballs were banned in 1920.

Softball, a game mainly for nonprofessionals, developed at the same time. Although the origins are obscure, credit is usually given to George Hancock of Chicago, who was inspired by the rowdy play of friends in 1887. One man threw a boxing glove at another who hit it back with a broomstick. Hancock made up rules, but they remained subject to many local changes. In 1933 the Amateur Softball Association formed and began to standardize the rules, including the size of the ball (12-inch circumference). Today some 40 million Americans play the game and most use slow pitch rules. This means that the batter has a greater chance of hitting the ball. Women and girls participated from the beginning, and softball has become a varsity sport for women in college. It is one of the most social and least commercialized of American sports.

Astrodome: To Cover a Baseball Field

One of the great goals of architecture throughout history has been to enclose ever larger volumes of space. This age-old quest achieved a milestone with the building of the Astrodome, the most innovative stadium since the time of the ancient Roman Colosseum. According to Roy M. Hofheinz, the man who turned the thought into reality, his idea of an air-conditioned stadium came from the old Colosseum. When the Romans constructed the Colosseum in the 1st century A.D., they used awnings to keep out the hot sun, and fountains to cool the air. Hofheinz, a Houston millionaire, led a group of investors who acquired a major league baseball franchise for his home city in 1960. He promised the National League that the owners would build a new stadium. "If those Romans could put a lid on their stadium, so can we," he figured.

Hofheinz consulted engineers, architects, and Houston businessmen. He won approval of his plans from Houston area voters, who supplied most of the money. The new home of the Houston Astros, the Astrodome, opened in 1965 and cost $45 million to build. The roof was a flat, elongated arch with a clear span of 642 feet. It was 218 feet above the ground, higher than a fly ball could be hit. It was made of a double layer of clear plastic sheets to let in sunlight and provide insulation. Inside there was an air-conditioning system designed to hold the temperature at 72 degrees and filter out smoke.

Six circular, colorful tiers of seats rose above the green playing field of Bermuda grass. Spectators entered at mid-level and had a choice of cushioned seats. There were no obstructions of view and all seats pointed toward second base. At the top was a ring of blue skyboxes where large groups could enjoy television, lounge chairs, and kitchen facilities. Most impressive was a 474-foot-long scoreboard that could flash commercials, lead cheers, and keep score. When an Astro player hit a home run, the scoreboard would flash rockets, blow whistles, ring bells, and feature cowboys firing bullets that would ricochet from side to side. The stadium could seat 45,000 fans for baseball and 52,000 for football. It could be used for many different activities, even for tennis matches.

The day before the first baseball game, however, the architects and athletes discovered an enormous problem. When a pop fly was hit, the fielders could not see the white ball as it arched against a background of steel girders and the daylight glare of the plastic roof. The outfielders began wearing batting helmets and holding their arms over their heads as the balls dropped around them. The difficulty ended when workmen painted the outside of the dome. Then, however, the grass died because it did not receive enough sunlight. Hofheinz solved that problem by installing a carpet of artificial grass just invented by Chemstrand. This was the beginning of AstroTurf, a synthetic surface that has been used in outdoor as well as indoor stadiums. There has been significant controversy over AstroTurf vs. natural turf, with proponents of each arguing about tradition, beauty, and safety.

The Astrodome was comfortable and exciting; even conservative players admitted its success. It introduced not only covered, air-conditioned stadiums for field sports but also large scoreboards, skyboxes, comfortable padded seats for fans, and artificial playing surfaces. Some purists objected to the control of weather, and others disliked the artificial playing surface. At present, there is a trend to one-sport, open-air stadiums. Nonetheless, even if a stadium planner rejects the idea, no one can overlook the example of the Astrodome when constructing a new stadium. Other cities followed the Houston example, and the graceful domes have softened the jagged office skylines of North American cities.

This interior shot of the Houston Astrodome, the most innovative stadium since the Roman Colosseum, was taken with a "fish-eye" camera lens. Shadows on the field are removed by more than 4,500 skylights with light-diffusing surfaces.

The early professional baseball stadiums were located on cheap land at the end of trolley car lines and were made of wood. Some seats were under a cover that provided shade, while the rest were exposed to the "bleaching" effect of sun and rain. The "bleachers" became the cheap seats of the stadium. Average crowds amounted to 4,000 fans, but in 1897 some 25,000 showed up for a game between Baltimore and Boston. The fans covered the outfield, and the umpires ruled that any ball hit into the crowd was an automatic double. Boston won 19-10. In 1908, Jack Norworth, who worked on vaudeville stages, wrote "Take Me Out to the Ballgame," which became the unofficial anthem of baseball fans around the country.

As the U.S. population increased, the growing cities demanded more baseball. Some teams prospered and better stadiums were built, such as Tiger Stadium in Detroit in 1912, Fenway Park of Boston in 1912, Wrigley Field in Chicago in 1914, and Yankee Stadium in New York in 1923. Especially after 1960, major-league expansion brought another wave of stadium construction, and no stadium was more innovative than the Astrodome of Houston, Texas, which opened in 1965.

In 1899, Ban Johnson renamed his Western League the American League and moved teams into Cleveland, Detroit, and Chicago to compete with the National League. After several years of fighting, the two organizations signed a truce in 1903.

To deal with a sticky climate of high humidity and high temperature, the people of Harris County, which surrounded Houston, voted to build a baseball park that was enclosed and air-conditioned. Although, according to engineers, this was possible, it had never been done. Under the leadership of Judge Roy Hofheinz, part owner of the Houston Astros, the stadium was constructed. It worked well but had to have an artificial playing surface in place of grass, which would not grow indoors. Hofheinz called the new surface "AstroTurf." Since that time, in cities where weather is a problem, such as New Orleans, Seattle, Minneapolis, San Antonio, and Toronto, domed stadiums have been built. Because of their high cost, domed stadiums were often used for more than one sport; the trend is now toward single-sport facilities such as Camden Yards, which was built for baseball in Baltimore in 1992.

To control the schedules, rules, and business of baseball, two major leagues developed. William A. Hulbert of Chicago brought together owners from Boston, Chicago, Cincinnati, Louisville, Hartford, St. Louis, New York, and Philadelphia in 1876 to form the National League. The league gave each team a franchise, territorial rights to their city; agreed to a 50-cents admission charge; and set up a schedule of five home games and five away games. The league owners also disciplined the players. When four players from Louisville admitted to throwing games in 1877 for gamblers, the National League expelled the players for life. The same punishment was imposed in 1921–22 when eight Chicago White Sox players "fixed" the 1919 World Series.

In 1879 the owners developed a "reserve" agreement to stop players from moving from one team to another. Star players could be held in reserve; they were allowed no contracts from other teams. By 1887 the reserve clause, as it was called, had been extended to cover almost all members of the team. The reserve clause essentially gave a team lifetime rights to any player it signed to a contract. Needless to say, the inability to sign with any team that desired a player's services limited a player's freedom and kept his wages low. After long agitation and court challenges, the reserve clause was modified in 1976 to permit players with six years of major-league experience to become free agents. The athlete could then sign a new contract with any team.

Compared to other American baseball clubs, teams in the National League survived and prospered. The league met challenges from other groups, including organizations formed by the players themselves. In 1894, however, Byron Bancroft "Ban" Johnson became president of the Western League, which was made up of minor teams in the central United States. In 1899 Johnson changed the name of his group to the American League, and moved teams into Detroit, Chicago, and Cleveland to compete with the National League.

After several years of competition, the two organizations signed a truce in 1903. They made room for each other, respected each other's franchises and reserve clauses, and played the first World Series. In that year Boston beat Philadelphia. The next year, 1904, there was no series because the National League champion, the New York Giants, refused to play. Fiery John McGraw, the manager, had had trouble with "Ban" Johnson and sniffed that he would not play against a team from "a minor-league aggregation." In 1905 the World Series started again and has continued every year since then with the exception of 1994, when a player's strike prematurely ended the baseball season.

The history of baseball is filled with statistics and records, heroes and goats. It is impossible to note everything, but three players—Ty Cobb, Babe Ruth, and Jackie Robinson—deserve special mention for their role in history. During his 24 years in the major leagues, Tyrus Raymond "Ty" Cobb (1886–1961) was not only the most feared man in baseball but probably the best player as well. During his career, Cobb had a lifetime batting average of .367 (calculated by dividing the number of base hits by the number of times at bat) and scored 2,246 runs. These are records that still hold. He was a ferocious base runner who had a reputation of sharpening his spikes to intimidate the defensive players. "When I played ball, I didn't play for fun," he said. "It's no pink tea, and mollycoddlers had better stay out. It's a contest and everything that implies, a struggle for supremacy, a survival of the fittest."

Cobb was thoroughly disliked. He ate alone, roomed alone, and once jumped into the stands to beat up a crippled heckler who had no hands. His early teammates broke his bats, nailed his uniform to the wall, and locked him in the bathroom. Cobb's ugly behavior supposedly came from his difficult youth in Georgia. His mother mistakenly killed his demanding father with a shotgun. She thought that he was an

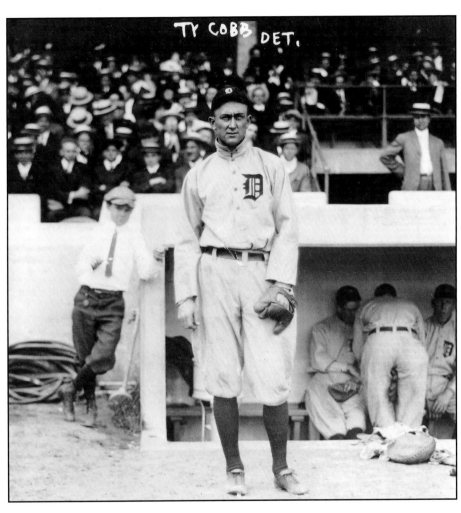

intruder, and the event apparently became a painful memory for the young ballplayer. Nonetheless, the "Georgia Peach," as he was called, was the first choice of voters when the Baseball Hall of Fame began inducting players in 1936.

Cobb's extraordinarily high batting average stemmed from his ability to hit the ball to places in the field where it was difficult to catch. This was particularly important in the "dead ball" era before 1920. The same baseball was used throughout a game, and they were not well-made. They became lop-sided, stained by grass and tobacco juice, soggy, and difficult to hit for

Ty Cobb used to sharpen his spikes to intimidate the opposing team. Thoroughly disliked by his teammates—and some fans—Cobb was the first choice of voters when the Baseball Hall of Fame began in 1936.

any great distance. The ball was "dead" rather than lively, and thus important to place as Cobb did.

The ball had attained its standard circumference of 9 inches in 1871, and over time other gradual changes were made. Cowhide covers replaced sheepskin, taut yarn replaced loose windings, and cork centers replaced rubber in 1910. The stitch design became standard, as did the white color. By 1920 the ball could be hit harder and farther because it was better made. Umpires, moreover, began to use more than one ball per game. The lighter "jack rabbit" ball, as it was called, made possible the home run style of Babe Ruth.

George Herman "Babe" Ruth (1895–1948) was the player best known and remembered by the public. Born in Baltimore, Ruth grew up and learned to play baseball in the St. Mary's Industrial Home for Boys. In 1914, he began as a talented, left-handed pitcher for the Baltimore Orioles, shortly switched to the Red Sox, turned to a hitting career, and in 1920 started playing for the New York Yankees. The "Sultan of Swat," as sportswriter Grantland Rice called him, swung his heavy 44-ounce bat for home runs, and hit them often. The fans cheered when he hit and groaned when he missed. Attendance at Yankee games increased from 600,000 to 1,000,000 per year after Ruth arrived. When Yankee Stadium was finished in 1923 it was called "the House that Ruth Built." In 1927 he set a home run record of 60 for a season. Roger Maris of the Yankees finally broke this record in 1961 with 61 home runs, but in a season that was eight games longer. Interestingly, Maris received some

fan abuse for his achievement; they did not like the thought of anyone being better than Ruth.

The secret to Ruth's success with the fans was that he came from a humble background and had an outgoing personality. He was easy to like. Ruth truly loved kids and spent hours visiting sick children and signing autographs without charge. He lived heartily, and once ate 18 eggs and 8 soda pops for breakfast. The uninhibited Ruth liked to party all night—something the press at the time did not report. His roommate Ping Bodie commented, "I don't room with Ruth. I room with his suitcase." Asked how he knew what to hit, Ruth replied, "All I can tell 'em is I pick a good one and sock it. I get back to the dugout and they ask me what it was I hit and I tell 'em I don't know except it looked good."

The most famous incident involving Ruth was the "called shot" in the third game of the 1932 World Series between the Yankees and the Chicago Cubs. In the game the Cub players were shouting insults at Ruth while he was at bat and Ruth wanted to zing a foul ball into their dugout. With the crowd booing and throwing lemons, one of which rolled across the plate, the Yankee raised first one finger, then two fingers to indicate the strikes against him. Ruth then smacked a slow, low curve ball into the center field stands for a home run. That silenced the crowd. Only one newspaper reporter said that Ruth had pointed to where he would hit the ball and then did it. That report and later ones, however, spawned the legend that the Yankee slugger had called the shot. Ruth told Chicago sportswriter John Carmichael, "I didn't exactly point to any spot. All I wanted to do was give that thing a ride out of the park, anywhere."

Because of declining ability, Ruth was released by the Yankees in 1934. He played briefly for the Boston Braves and then permanently retired in 1935 with a batting average of .342 for 22 seasons. Hank Aaron finally surpassed Ruth's career record of 714 home runs in 1974. Christy Walsh, who became Ruth's business agent in 1921, put part of Ruth's earnings into annuities, an investment that gave the spendthrift Ruth a steady income during his older days. When Ruth died of throat cancer in 1948, Grantland Rice, one of the great sports journalists, wrote, "May the great umpire rule him safe at home."

Compared to Ruth or Cobb, Jack Roosevelt "Jackie" Robinson (1919–72) does not have particularly impressive statistics. He played nine seasons for the Brooklyn Dodgers at second base and batted .311. What Robinson accomplished for American society, however, was of immense importance. He was the first black player in modern major league baseball; he was the athlete who broke the color line in America's most important sport.

The time had come by 1947. Until this moment the black citizens of the United States, especially in the South, usually lived in isolated housing areas; ate at black-owned restaurants; attended separate schools; and played on all-black athletic teams. They were allowed to associate with the majority white community mainly in the area of business. In the South, there were individual drinking fountains for the white and black races in public places. Even on buses

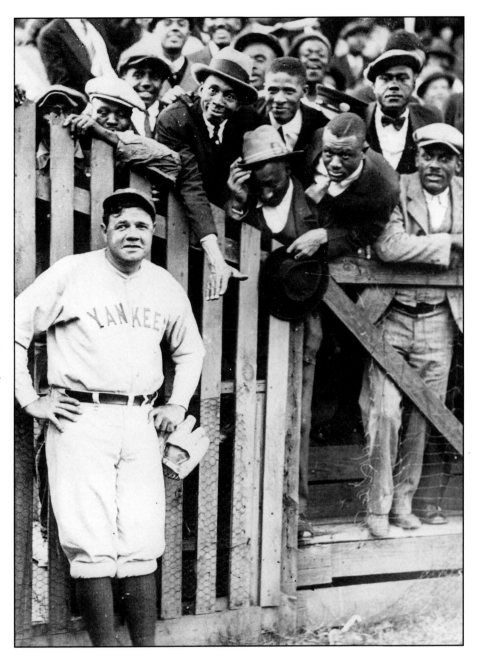

blacks were forced to sit at the back. The division of the races was enforced by Jim Crow laws, local ordinances to enforce racial separation. The National Association for the Advancement of Colored People (NAACP) began to ask for an end to this segregation as early as 1909. During World War II, blacks, albeit in separate units, fought for the safety of the United States and the world. It became obviously illogical to oppose the prejudice of Adolf Hitler and the Nazis, and yet allow such prejudice to exist at home.

In New York City, Fiorello La Guardia (1882–1947), who was mayor from 1933 to 1945, appointed a commission during the

Attendance at New York Yankee games increased from 600,000 to 1 million per year after Babe Ruth arrived in 1920. Fans loved his down-to-earth personality.

Jackie Robinson broke the ban against blacks playing major league baseball in 1947. Here, Robinson throws to first base as Marty Marion of the St. Louis Cardinals slides into second.

war to study race relations in the city. Discrimination in sports was one of the topics of concern. The committee included Branch Rickey (1881–1965), who had become the general manager and part-owner of the Brooklyn Dodgers in 1943. New York had a large black population, and Rickey thought that black athletes would help his team. "The Negroes will make us winners for years to come, and for that I will happily bear being called a bleeding heart and a do-gooder and all that humanitarian rot," he told his family.

Rickey chose Jackie Robinson as the person to integrate blacks into baseball. Robinson was a fine all-around athlete from the University of California at Los Angeles who had been an army lieutenant during World War II. In 1945 he was playing shortstop for the Kansas City Monarchs, an important black baseball team. Rickey signed Robinson to play with the Montreal Royals, a Dodger farm club, in 1946. He then brought the black player to the Dodgers in 1947. Rickey warned the combative young man to avoid the confrontations that would occur with fans and other players. Robinson said, "Mr. Rickey, do you want a ball-player who's afraid to fight back?" Rickey replied, "I want a player with guts enough not to fight back."

Robinson held his temper for two years as he agreed to do and let his superior athletic skills at bat, running bases, and in the infield speak for all black people. He started at first base, led the Dodgers to a pennant victory, and won the first major league Rookie of the Year award. Black fans flooded the stadiums and ended the remnants of segregation in the stands. Robinson moved to second base in 1948, agitated for more black players and managers in sports, and retired in 1957. He had opened the door for black athletes and helped bring to an end segregation in sports. It was a grand accomplishment in sports and for society. Because of this courageous athlete, segregation in American sports died at second base.

During Robinson's day, baseball was the nation's most important sport. This was one

Grantland Rice, pictured here at the NBC microphone in 1930, was one of the leading sportswriters of the 1920s.

reason for his great impact. Baseball had grown up with American cities and flourished in an industrial society that needed entertainment. The technological improvements of the nation supported this development. Railroads carried teams from town to town. Reports of teams' successes, or failures, were transmitted to hometown fans over the telegraph and telephone wires, and printed in cheap local newspapers. Sports reporting began in the 1880s, but sections and pages dedicated to athletics did not become standard until the 1920s.

Sports reporting featured a special type of writing. The journalism tended to be exaggerated, melodramatic, and riddled with references to life and death, war and combat. It was entertaining and fun to read. Rather than confront the misery and difficulties spelled out on the front pages, many people chose to turn to the sports section first. Here they read the lines of journalists like Grantland Rice (1880–1954) of the *New York Tribune*, who was the foremost sportswriter between the world wars. "When the one Great Scorer comes to write against your name, he marks—not whether you won or lost—but how you played the game," he wrote toward the end of his poem, "Alumnus Football," in 1908. It was a philosophy of life and a comfort to everyone who had lost in sports contests.

Beyond the print media, motion pictures and radio also popularized sports and baseball. Movies appeared at the turn of the century and often presented sports as a part of a news "short" before the main feature in the theaters. The new radio technology appeared in 1920, and on November 25, 1920, WTAW in College Station, Texas,

broadcast a play-by-play description of the Thanksgiving Day football game between the University of Texas and Texas A&M. Two million people listened to the 1923 heavyweight fight between Jess Willard and Louis Firpo, and in 1926 a 23-station network carried the games of the World Series. Graham McNamee (1888–1942), a former opera singer, became the first star of sports announcing. He described the action of football, baseball, boxing, horse racing, and other sports with emotional excitement. He let his voice speed up at fast-moving moments, slow down in others. He projected his personality and provided analysis. After his 1925 World Series broadcast, he received 50,000 fan letters. McNamee was followed by Bill Stern, who announced for NBC from 1939 to 1952, and Walter L.

"Red" Barber, who became the voice of the Brooklyn Dodgers in 1939 and then the New York Yankees from 1953 to 1966. Barber used expressions from his native Mississippi, such as "sittin' in the catbird seat," which meant to be in a good position.

In the 1940s, among the most popular announcers was Jay Hanna "Dizzy" Dean (1911–74). During the 1930s, Dean had been a star pitcher for the St. Louis Cardinals, but he ruined his arm by throwing with a broken toe. He retired into the broadcast booth and became a fan favorite with his ungrammatical speech and good humor. He once explained that he had reached only the second grade in school, and added, "I didn't do so good in first grade either." He was noted for such statements as: "He slud into third," "He's standing confidentially at the plate," and "Don't forget to miss tomorrow's game." At slow moments during the baseball games, he would give recipes for black-eyed peas, or sing verses of "The Wabash Cannonball." Dean made a successful transition from radio to television in the 1950s and retired in the 1960s.

The first televised sporting event in America was a baseball game between Princeton and Columbia universities in May 1939 in New York City. It was announced by Bill Stern, but not many people watched. There were only 400 receiving sets in town. That telecast was followed, however, several days later by a bicycle race, and in June with a boxing match. In the same year the Mutual Broadcasting System paid $2,500 to show the National Football League championship game. This start of television was interrupted by World War II, but the potential for entertainment and payment of money for the right to broadcast had been demonstrated. It was an indication of the future.

After World War II, television gave a new dimension to sports. Television networks paid athletic organizations for the right to broadcast events, and corporations paid the networks for the right to display commercials for their products. Television revenues became enormously important to teams. For example, television sports contracts from 1990 to 1994 amounted to $3.6 billion. The medium affected times of games, length of events, how people viewed the action, and the popularity of various sports. Television created interest in sports and tapped into a latent desire for athletic entertainment. In 1979, when the Entertainment

Sports Programming Network (ESPN) began all-sports broadcasting, one of the founders commented, "We believe the appetite for sports in this country is insatiable." He seems to have been correct.

One important figure in television development was Roone Arledge, who joined the American Broadcasting Company (ABC) in 1960 after producing an award-winning children's program on the Columbia Broadcasting System (CBS) in 1959. As the head of sports broadcasting, Arledge wanted to involve the unseen television viewer in the action. He placed cameras on cranes and blimps; he used close-up shots of athletes and coaches; he used microphones to catch the sound of punts and the roar of the crowd; he ordered camera views of fans and cheerleaders. The Dallas Cowboy Cheerleaders became as famous as the team. The creative Arledge also started the *Wide World of Sports* in 1961 to explore athletic activity around the world. Sports enthusiasts everywhere learned to recite his opening lines: "Spanning the globe to bring you the constant variety of sport, the thrill of victory, the agony of defeat, the human drama of athletic competition."

In 1968 ABC became the first American network to televise the Olympics, and two years later Arledge started *Monday Night Football*. Previously, professional games had been telecast only on Sundays. Arledge brought together a team of three experts to analyze the games and thus boosted the career of the most famous, and annoying, sportscaster of all time—Howard Cosell (1920–95). While practicing law, Cosell began doing five-minute sports broadcasts

for ABC in 1955. He presented a television special about Babe Ruth in 1962 and began to make appearances on *Wide World of Sports*. From 1966 to 1973, he announced boxing for the network and courageously took the side of Muhammad Ali when the fighter refused induction into the army in 1967. He worked the broadcast booth for *Monday Night Football* for 13 years. "Tell it like it is," was his motto, but many fans turned off the sound because they could stand neither his arrogance, nor his grating voice with its Brooklyn accent. Cosell was an announcer that people loved to hate. In the books he wrote after retirement, Cosell managed to offend even his fellow broadcasters. As comedian Buddy Hackett said, "Some hated him like poison, and some just hated him regular."

Television with Cosell and others, however, shifted the enthusiasm of fans from baseball to football. Football with its periodic action of stops and starts—huddle, play, tackle, huddle—was ideal for commercials. Announcers explained plays and viewers became more knowledgeable about the sport. Football replaced baseball as the most popular sport to watch. In 1961 viewers preferred baseball over football by 34 percent to 21 percent. By 1972, the public had shifted preference to football from baseball by 36 percent to 21 percent. Another study of the TV audience from 1979 to 1983 revealed 28 percent watching football and only 7.2 percent looking at baseball. A change had occurred and football was now America's national sport. As journalist Mary McGrory of the *Washington Post* observed, "Baseball is what we were, football is what we have become."

Football appealed to the middle class. It was like the corporate world where they worked. The sport was bound by time—timeouts, quarters, halftime, delay of game penalties. Life also was time-bound, mortal. Football, in addition, was rational, coordinated, and complex like business. The success of the game depended on teamwork, but also allowed for individual stars. There was an element of luck, just as in life. The violence on the field was a relief to the fan whose life was controlled by business and society. It was a sport created by the middle class in their colleges, and became the national sport as people increasingly entered the middle class through a rising standard of living.

Rowing was the earliest college sport in both the United States and England. Large crowds of spectators gathered along the riverbanks to watch the first racing sculls made of cedar wood. Harvard raced Oxford on the Thames River in England in 1869, and lost. The American schools tended to emulate the schools in Great Britain and absorbed the amateur ideal along with rugby and soccer. Intramural games between classes, particularly freshmen against sophomores, were common at the eastern schools. The rules were not solid, however, and when McGill University of Montreal played two games against Harvard in 1874 the players changed the rules for each game. McGill played a form of rugby, and Harvard liked to throw and strike the ball with the hand. In 1875 Yale and Harvard played a game combining rules of soccer and rugby. The next year Columbia, Harvard, Princeton, and Yale formed the Intercollegiate Football Association (IFA) to play

games with each other that resembled rugby. There was no long tradition of rugby in the United States, and indeed, the rules had been only recently formulated in England.

The rules began to change in the United States in 1880, mainly due to the interest of Walter C. Camp (1859–1925) of Yale. He was a student at Yale from 1875 to 1882, played on the athletic teams, and took a job in a New Haven watch factory in 1882. He became an unpaid coach at Yale and its representative to the IFA. Camp, "the father of American football," began suggesting and obtaining rule changes that defined the new sport. Rugby and soccer were continuous action games. In rugby, when a player went down with the ball the teams fought for possession in a mass effort called a "scrum," or "scrummage." This was a 15th-century English word meaning a bout with swords, or "skirmish."

In 1880 Camp suggested stopping the play when a man went down and allowing him to kick the ball back to his quarterback from a "line of scrimmage." This was a "down," which stopped the continuous action of play. He also obtained a reduction in team members on the field from 15 to 11. In 1882, he recommended three downs for a team to go five yards; and a scoring system

Cambridge University (left foreground) beat Oxford (right) in this boat race by covering the course from Putney to Mortlake in 17:50, breaking the previous record. The teams have just passed under the Hammersmith Bridge on the Thames River in London.

This football game took place around the turn of the century. Note that the players wear relatively little protective equipment—not even helmets—compared to today.

that allowed 2 points for a touchdown, 4 points for the goal kick after a touchdown (now called the conversion or extra-point kick), and 5 points for a field goal. To keep track of the downs the field had to be marked. Originally, it was crisscrossed with straight lines going both length and breadth, or in a "gridiron" pattern. The football field has since dropped the length lines, but the term *gridiron* remains.

Football spread across the country through the colleges and raised questions about violence. After 18 high school and college students died on the field in 1905, President Theodore Roosevelt called representatives from Harvard, Princeton, and Yale to the White House for a discussion of the problem. Nothing was accomplished, however, until Henry B. McCracken, the chancellor of New York University, lost another student in the NYU–Union College game. He called for change, and late in 1905 representatives from 62 colleges met to form the Intercollegiate Athletic Association. This organization, which became the National Collegiate Athletic Association (NCAA), in 1910 took over responsibility for the rules of college football.

In 1906, the NCAA designated three downs to go 10 yards and legalized the forward pass. An incomplete pass, however, drew a 15-yard penalty. In 1910, the NCAA abolished interlocking interference, whereby players locked arms as they ran down the field; required seven offensive

men to be placed on the line of scrimmage; and eliminated the penalty for passing. The regulation for seven men on the line of scrimmage eliminated the "flying wedge" formation, in which 10 players formed a "V" and plowed over the defenders. The force of the wedge caused injuries. In 1912, the NCAA allowed 4 downs for 10 yards and 6 points for scoring a touchdown. The length of the field was placed at 100 yards, with end zones 10 yards deep. The field goal had been changed to three points in 1909. The circumference of the ball also changed in 1912 from 27 inches to 23 inches. It is now 21 and one-half inches. Before the ball changed, it was thrown end-over-end. With the oblong shape, the players could throw a spiral pass that was much more accurate. The outline of the modern game was thus drawn.

The potential of the pass play was demonstrated when Notre Dame defeated Army 35-14 in 1913. Knute Rockne (1888–1931), then a student at Notre Dame, practiced receiving passes from his friend, quarterback Gus Dorais, during the summer. They surprised Army, but the cadets used the new weapon to defeat their archrival, Navy, later in the season. After graduation, Rockne became an assistant coach at Notre Dame, and then head coach in 1918. During the next 13 years, Rockne directed five undefeated seasons for the Irish. He became noted for his inspirational pep talks, the most famous of which involved "the Gipper."

George Gipp, one of his stars, had died at the end of the 1920 season of a throat infection and pneumonia. Supposedly, as he died he said to Coach Rockne, "When

Notre Dame football coach Knute Rockne rallied his team in 1928 with the inspirational story of his friend George Gipp. "Let's win one just for the Gipper," he said.

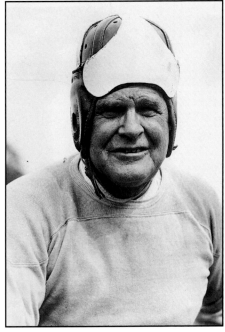

Glenn "Pop" Warner, head football coach of Temple University, wears the leather helmet that became common after 1910. On this day in 1933, "Pop" led his squad in the first practice of the season.

things are wrong and the breaks are beating the boys, tell them to go in there with all they've got and win one just for the Gipper." In 1928, with Notre Dame tied with Army at halftime 0-0, Rockne asked the team to win for the Gipper. In the second half the Irish won 12-6. Rockne died in an airplane crash in 1931.

Inventive, successful coaches like Rockne became as well-known as their star players. Glenn S. "Pop" Warner (1871–1954), who worked at Georgia, Cornell, Pittsburgh, Carlisle Institute, Stanford, and Temple in 44 years of coaching, invented the single-wing formation, which placed the majority of players on one side of the ball. The formation was perfected by Coach Bernie Bierman, known as "the Silver Fox of the Northland," at the University of Minnesota in the 1930s. While instructing at Stanford in 1940, Clark D. "Chuck"

Shaughnessy (1892–1970) analyzed his talent and reinvented the T-formation, which dated back to 1906 and had fallen into disuse. He used speed and deception to replace the power of the single wing. The backs lined up straight across behind the quarterback, who took the ball in a snap underneath the legs of the center. It became the basic formation for most modern offensive patterns.

The most influential coach, however, came from the professional ranks. The Green Bay Packers had not had a winning season for a decade when Vincent T. Lombardi (1913–70) arrived as head coach in 1959. "I have never been on a losing team, gentlemen, and I don't intend to start now," he announced at the first team meeting. He won five championships, including the first two Super Bowls. Lombardi was a perfectionist and paid attention to details.

Vince Lombardi displays one of his two Super Bowl rings. He told his Green Bay Packers, "Winning is not a sometime thing here, it is an all-the-time thing."

Samuel "Slingin' Sammy" Baugh honed his passing skills by throwing the ball through a tire swinging at the end of a rope. He is considered to be football's first modern passer.

He made his men practice the same plays repeatedly until there were no mistakes.

The phrase, "Winning isn't everything, it's the only thing," has been attributed, perhaps incorrectly, to Lombardi. But he could not stand to lose and said to his players, "Winning is not a sometime thing here, it is an all-the-time thing." Important was the concentration on winning, a philosophy of sports that at the current time has replaced the earlier sentiment of Grantland Rice, ". . . not whether you won or lost, but how you played the game."

Professional football began in 1920 with the formation of the American Professional Football Association at the meeting of 10 team owners in an automobile showroom in Canton, Ohio. The organization was made up mainly of small-town groups using semiprofessional players who worked all week at other jobs. Membership in the league fluctuated as teams went out of existence and others formed. George Hallas, owner of the Decatur Staleys, moved to Chicago and renamed his team the Bears. He did this because the Chicago Cubs baseball team was so popular. The same year, 1922, he suggested that the organization change its name to the National Football League. Slowly the rest of the teams, with the exception of Green Bay, followed Hallas's lead and moved to the big cities.

Still, professional football sputtered. It gained somewhat in popularity when Harold E. "Red" Grange (1903–91) joined the Chicago Bears as a single-wing running back. Grange had been a sensational player at the University of Illinois, and Grantland Rice had nicknamed him "the Galloping Ghost of the Gridiron." In 1924 against

Michigan he scored the first four times he touched the football and had to lean against the goalposts to rest. That day he ran for a total of 402 yards and made five touchdowns in a 39-14 victory.

Five days after his final college game in 1925, he dropped out of school and joined the Chicago Bears. Grange commented, "I'm out to get the money and I don't care who knows it. My advice to everybody is to get to the gate while the getting's good." Grange's presence at Wrigley Field brought out 35,000 fans, seven times the usual number. He continued to attract crowds, but missed the 1928 season with a torn tendon. He was unable to play as well after that. "I was just another halfback," he said. He was named to the first all-professional team in 1931, retired from football in 1933, and became a successful sports announcer.

More important for the future of professional football, however, was Samuel A. "Slingin' Sammy" Baugh. He was born in Tyler, Texas, and attended college at Texas Christian University in the mid-1930s. Too slight in build to be a running back, Baugh concentrated on passing and kicking. He honed his passing skills by throwing the ball through a tire swinging at the end of a rope. After turning the Southwest Conference into an aerial circus, Baugh joined the Washington Redskins in 1937. He played for the Redskins for 16 seasons, first as a single-wing tailback who led the league in passing, punting, and interceptions in 1943. The next year Baugh moved to quarterback when the Redskins installed the T-formation. He directed his team to two championships and five division titles, but his significance was as the first modern

passer. After "Slingin' Sammy," the professional game belonged to the quarterback who could throw well.

Professional football, however, did not become deeply popular with the American people until after World War II. Television money negotiated by the league and shared among the teams helped bring about the change. "What Rozelle [commissioner of the NFL from 1960 to 1989] did with television receipts probably saved football at Green Bay," said Vince Lombardi. Television also saved the upstart American Football League, which challenged the NFL in 1960. Frustrated by the lack of NFL franchises, oil millionaires Lamar Hunt of Dallas and K. S. "Bud" Adams of Houston organized a new league with teams in Boston, Buffalo, Dallas, Denver, Houston, Los Angeles, New York, and Oakland. This started a war between the leagues.

Unable to obtain a contract to show NFL games in 1964, the National Broadcasting Company (NBC) signed a $42 million agreement with the new league. The next year the New York Jets signed Joe Willie Namath, a quarterback from the University of Alabama, for $420,000 paid over three years. The unprecedented salary made Namath a celebrity and started the trend to large contracts for athletes that reached multimillion dollar levels in the 1990s. Television revenue made it possible. Namath was worth every penny, however. Jets ticket sales doubled as the press reported every move of the personable, long-haired quarterback on and off the field.

The NFL finally made peace with the AFL. The merger of the two leagues resulted in the Super Bowl, which began in 1967 and matched the champions of the two leagues. Green Bay won the first two Super Bowls, but Namath led the Jets to victory, 16-7, over the Baltimore Colts in Super Bowl III. "We're going to win. I guarantee it!" announced "Broadway Joe" before the game. He made the prediction come true with patient, accurate passing. The victory confounded the critics, who thought the AFL was too weak to compete with the NFL. The AFL proved with Super Bowl III, however, that its teams could provide exciting football and championship performance.

Canada also developed its version of U.S.-style football. The changes from rugby to football were similar, although delayed about 20 years. Frank "Shag" Shaughnessy, who had played at Notre Dame, became coach at McGill University in Montreal in 1912. He was the first football coach in Canada and played a role similar to that of Walter Camp at Yale. Shaughnessy agitated for rule changes that pushed the Canadians toward the United States version of the game. Still, there were differences. Canadian football used 12 players, which provided an extra backfield man. The five backs were allowed greater motion before the ball was snapped, and the field was 110 yards long with end zones 25 yards deep. Teams were

Weeb Eubank (left), head coach of the New York Jets, keeps a sharp eye on Joe Namath, the team's quarterback, in June 1965. Namath tests his left knee, for which he underwent surgery six months before this photo was taken.

allowed only three downs, rather than U.S. football's four, to move 10 yards. The result was that Canadian football encouraged more passing plays. The slight difference in rules, however, did not deter U.S. players from migrating to Canada. With the merger of several groups, the Canadian Football League (CFL) began in 1956.

Although there have been attempts to popularize football beyond Canada and the United States, the efforts have faltered. This has not been true for another American sports invention, basketball, which has gained worldwide popularity. The game sprang from the mind of James Naismith (1861–1939) in 1891, while he was an instructor at the School for Christian Workers, later called the International YMCA Training School, in Springfield, Massachusetts. The Young Men's Christian Association (YMCA) was a global organization that embraced the idea that physical as well as religious training was important for human beings. Born near Almonte, Ontario, Naismith had graduated from McGill University, and after leaving a Presbyterian seminary joined the YMCA school in Massachusetts. Luther H. Gulick, the director of the school, asked Naismith to design an interesting indoor sport for physical activity in a gymnasium during the winter. He thought that people were bored with calisthenics.

Naismith thought that a large ball thrown at a horizontal goal might be good. He rejected the idea of a vertical goal like that of soccer because the players would hurl the ball at it. He also did not like the idea of running with a ball because it might lead to tackling. He considered the thought of throwing a ball into a box, like the warm-up exercise he had used when he was captain of the McGill rugby team, but a box on the floor would be too easy. The box should be elevated so that scoring would be done with a soft, arched throw. There were no boxes available, but a janitor found some wooden peach baskets and nailed them to the lower railing of the gym's balcony, about 10 feet off the floor. Naismith used a soccer ball, divided his reluctant class into nine players each, dictated the rules, and tried the game. The janitor had to use a ladder to retrieve the ball every time it went into a basket, which was not very often. Basketball was thus born.

The sport was an immediate success and filtered rapidly through the YMCA network. Not only did it spread across the United States and Canada, but also to China, India, France, and England in 1895; Japan in 1900; and Persia in 1901. Americans took the game abroad during World War I. By 1940 basketball was played in 75 countries. Rules varied with facilities and interpretations. Clara Baer, a physical education teacher at Newcomb College in New Orleans, for example, received instructions from Naismith through the mail in 1895. She misunderstood the diagrams and thought the positions were stationary. She thus developed six-person team basketball for girls that required passing from zones. Baer called it "basquette ball," and it endured in some rural schools until 1995. Today, however, women play by rules generally similar to the men's game.

There was a certain amount of tinkering with the invention, especially in the early years: 20-minute halves in 1893; free throw

for fouls in 1894; the dribble, or bounce while running, in 1896; a field goal of two points in 1896; five-minute overtimes in 1907. Teams varied in size from 3 to 40, but Naismith and Gulick standardized the number at 5 in 1897. The peach baskets were replaced with wire buckets in 1892, but the ball still had to be poked out with a pole. In 1893 a cord netting was used with a pull chain that released the ball, but open-bottom nets were not approved until 1912. Backboards were made of wire mesh, and then wood. A photograph of a game in Madison Square Garden in New York City in 1934 shows a plate glass backboard in use. It improved visibility for the fans who sat behind the baskets, and glass backboards became common in the 1950s. The Overman Wheel Company provided the first basketball in 1894 to replace the soccer ball. In 1915 the AAU, YMCA, and NCAA met in order to standardize the rules.

College play remained within conferences until invitational tourneys began in New York's Madison Square Garden in 1934 during the Depression. Here, in 1936, Stanford's Hank Luisetti stunned other teams and stopped Long Island University with a running one-handed shot. He had developed the move as the only way of getting over larger players. It was unconventional for the time, however, because everyone else used a stationary two-handed push shot. Luisetti's innovation led to the single-handed jump shot used widely today. The Madison Square Garden meets evolved into the National Invitation Tournament (NIT) in 1938. It was considered the highest honor to play the NIT until gambling scandals in 1951 tarnished its image. After

that, the NCAA championships became most significant for colleges.

Other moves in basketball emerged from the hard, cement courts that cities built for urban recreation. Inner-city black players, in particular, emphasized speed, deception, and slam dunks. Arnold "Red" Auerbach, who was coach of the Boston Celtics from 1950 to 1966, and John R. Wooden, who was coach at the University of California at Los Angeles from 1950 to 1975, adopted elements of this new style of play. The teams of both coaches generally dominated the courts during the 1960s. This change coincided with the breakdown of segregation in southern colleges. On March 19, 1966, television viewers across the nation saw the all-black first string of Texas Western College of El Paso line up against the all-white first string of the University of Kentucky to play for the NCAA champi-

Basketball was popular with women and girls from the beginning. This team played at Bucknell University in Lewisburg, Pennsylvania, in 1896.

Sue Kelly in white and Anne Santorelli of St. John (15) try for the ball in the tipoff to this 1961 New York City–area high-school basketball game.

onship. Texas Western won 72-65. This was considered by historian Charles H. Martin as the "emancipation proclamation" for southern college basketball.

Girls' and women's basketball flourished in the early years of the game and then diminished. Two days after the invention of basketball, some female teachers who had heard the shouts of players coming from the gym, asked Naismith to instruct them. "When the time arrived," Naismith wrote later, "the girls appeared at the gymnasium, some with tennis shoes, but the majority with street clothes, costumes which were not made for freedom of movement. I shall never forget the sight that they presented in their long trailing dress with leg-of-mutton sleeves, and in several cases with a hint of a bustle." The YMCA hosted a tournament for women in 1892, and in 1896 the first intercollegiate game was played in Berkeley between the University of California and Stanford. No male spectators were allowed at the Berkeley match; it was considered improper for male viewers to attend.

In the first half of the 20th century most women physical education teachers did not believe that competition was good for girls. Sports were abandoned for "play days" that stressed social interaction. There was a belief that sports endangered female health.

Ethel Perrin, head of the women's division of the National Amateur Athletic Federation, commented in 1928: "The fact that a girl's nervous resistance cannot hold out under intensive physical strain is nature's warning." Male educators agreed and expanded their programs while the women retired to the bleachers and to the cheerleading squads.

The 1960s brought change, however. The feminist movement cast doubt on the passive image of women, and athletes like Billie Jean King demonstrated stunning female athletic ability. Consequently, rebel women educators formed first the Commission of Intercollegiate Athletics for Women in 1966, and then in 1971 the Association of Intercollegiate Athletics for Women (AIAW) to provide national athletic championships for women. The NCAA finally took over this function in 1981 and the AIAW ceased to operate in 1985.

Most important for this change of attitude about women athletics was Title IX of the Educational Amendments Act of 1972. The act was a result of the demand for equality of opportunity made by the civil rights and the feminist movements. Title IX read: "No person in the United States shall, on the basis of sex, be excluded from participation in, be denied the benefits of, or be subjected to discrimination under any

Six-foot-three-inch forward Carl Meinhold (23) of Long Island University outjumped six-foot-nine-inch center George Mikan (99) of De Paul University in this game at Madison Square Garden in New York City, 1945. De Paul won the game 74-47.

educational program or activity receiving federal financial assistance." Most colleges and many school districts received federal money. This simple statement meant essentially that equal effort and money should be devoted to women in athletic programs.

Title IX went into effect in 1975, and most colleges made an effort to conform. There was difficulty in budgeting, however, because no female sport cost nearly as much as football, an expensive male sport. The situation has remained basically unresolved even in the 1990s. At Division I schools of the NCAA in 1997, women's sports are funded at only one-third the amount given to men's sports. The change brought by Title IX, nonetheless, was dramatic. In 1971 there were 31,000 female varsity athletes in U.S. colleges; in 1995 there were 120,000. In the same period, high school female varsity athlete numbers changed from 294,000 to 2,400,000. Basketball, as well as other sports for women, became possible once more.

Professional basketball sputtered with little success before World War II, although a league formed in 1937, and barnstorming teams such as the Harlem Globetrotters (founded in 1927) provided professional entertainment. In 1946, however, the Chicago Gears signed George Mikan. After one season the Gears collapsed and Mikan went to play for the Minneapolis Lakers. At 6 feet 10 inches and 245 pounds, Mikan was the first basketball superstar. He had been drilled on short hook shots at DePaul University, where Coach Ray Meyer forced him to practice 250 shots per day with each hand. Mikan emerged from an awkward, glasses-wearing freshman to an All-Ameri-

can player. "It was like watching a flower bloom," said Meyer. Mikan was so dominating under the basket that the National Basketball Association (NBA) widened the foul lane from 6 to 12 feet in 1951 to try to neutralize him. After 9 seasons, 6 championships, and 10 broken bones, Mikan retired in 1956. Basketball was never the same after Mikan; everyone learned that good, big players were indispensable.

The most money that Mikan made during a season was $35,000, but with the advent of television professional basketball became much more popular and profitable

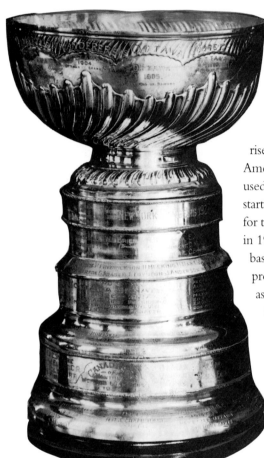

The Stanley Cup was originally donated to the Canadian Amateur Hockey Association by Sir Frederick Arthur Stanley to be a challenge cup for amateur teams. Most NHL players are Canadian, and the Montreal Canadiens have won the Cup a record 22 times.

for the players. The NBA came together in 1949 from the remains of two earlier leagues, the National Basketball League (1937–49) and the Basketball Association of America (1946–49). The popularity of professional basketball began a steady rise after 1960. A rival organization, the American Basketball Association, which used a patriotic red, white, and blue ball, started in 1967. It brought about a price war for top athletes and merged with the NBA in 1976. The development of professional basketball, with Mikan leading the way, provided opportunity for new stars such as Bob Cousy, Bill Russell, Wilt Chamberlain, and Michael Jordan.

From 1978 to 1981 Nancy Lieberman, a talented All-American basketball player from Old Dominion University, starred in the professional Women's Basketball League. Expenses were too high, however, and the league collapsed. Nonetheless, the idea of professional women's basketball did not die. In 1996 the American Basketball League began women's professional play, and in 1997 the Women's National Basketball Association (WNBA) started its first season. Backed by the NBA and television contracts, the WNBA began its playing schedule immediately after the NBA championships with the official slogan, "We Got Next." The slogan's reference to playground etiquette was an assertion that women's professional sports could no longer be denied.

One other popular spectator sport, hockey, deserves mention. Although a committee of the Amateur Hockey Association

of Canada proclaimed in 1941 that hockey was first played by soldiers of Her Majesty's Royal Canadian Rifles at Kingston, Canada, in 1855, there may be some doubt about the historical accuracy of this claim. Evidence of field hockey sports goes back to ancient Greece and Egypt. Traditional field sports, such as hurling in Scotland, may simply have moved to the ice in wintertime. The idea of ice skates are at least 2,000 years old. Two nine-man teams, nonetheless, played a game in 1875 at McGill University, and the first rules of ice hockey were written by McGill students in 1879. They were a combination of rules from lacrosse, polo, shinny, and rugby. The Amateur Hockey Association started in Canada in 1886. According to legend, someone made the first puck by slicing off the top and bottom of a round field hockey ball. The goalie was required to stand up because the puck always slid along the ice and a team could be prevented from scoring by simply lying down across the goal.

In 1893 the first Stanley Cup championship was held. The cup was presented by the governor general of the Dominion of Canada, Lord Stanley. In that same year hockey slipped southward across the United States border. The sport was introduced at Yale and Johns Hopkins universities, and in 1896 the United States Amateur Hockey League formed in New York City. A team from Seattle competed for the Stanley Cup in 1917, the same year that the National Hockey League (NHL) was established. A major expansion of the league, from 6 to 12 teams, occurred in 1967. More teams were added, and by 1994 there were 26 teams, 18 of which were located in the United States.

The league tinkered with the rules to make the game more interesting, particularly in the realm of penalty-box fouls and off-sides rules.

Hockey has been the least popular of the major professional sports, perhaps because the fast-moving puck is difficult to track on television. It has also developed a reputation in the United States as a violent sport where fighting is expected by the fans and the players. As comic Rodney Dangerfield commented in 1978, "I went to a fight the other night and a hockey game broke out." Fan loyalty is deep-rooted, nonetheless, particularly in Canada where ice hockey can be considered the national sport. It was an emotional calamity for the fans of the Edmonton Oilers when Wayne Gretzky, probably the best hockey player of all time, moved away from Canada to the Los Angeles Kings in 1988.

The game spread to Europe in the early 20th century and became an event of the Winter Olympics in 1924. Canada dominated the International Amateur Championships, which started in 1930, until Soviet players with precision playing began to win after World War II. From 1953 through 1972, the Soviets won 11 world titles while Canada won only 4. There was a controversy because Canada did not use its professional skaters, only amateurs. A showdown between the USSR and Canada came in 1972 when a team of Canadian NHL all-stars played a series of matches with the USSR, four games in Canada, four in Moscow. The Canadians won four to three, with one game tied. The Soviets, nonetheless, continued as a power-house in international hockey, and after the

fall of the Soviet Union in the late 1980s former Soviet players have been recruited to play on NHL teams.

The North American sports that have spread the farthest in the world seem to have been baseball, volleyball, and basketball. Baseball can be found around the Caribbean Sea and in the nations of the Far East. Volleyball spread through the YMCA network and is known almost everywhere. Around the world, basketball is viewed broadly on television, leagues flourish at many levels, and backstops with basketball hoops are universal. Ice hockey and football, which require expensive equipment and stadiums, have not gone much beyond Europe and North America. Therefore, it would seem that the reach of modern sports coincides, at least in part, with the past power of Great Britain and the present influence of the United States. Soccer and basketball have truly become the sports of the world.

Vlastimil Busnik (center foreground) of the 1952 Czechoslovakian Olympic hockey team tries to get the puck past goalie Ralph Hansch of the Canadian team during their Olympic match at Jordal Stadium in Oslo, Norway. The Canadians won the game 4-1.

OLYMPISKA SPELEN
STOCKHOLM 1912
29 JUNI — 22 JULI

A. BÖRTZELLS TR. A.B. STOCKHOLM

Chapter 7
The World of Sports

Jack Howard, the captain of the U.S. table tennis team that was visiting Japan for the world championships in April 1971, was asked by a Chinese official if the team might wish to tour China. "We have invited the Americans so that we can learn from each other and elevate our standards of play," said Sung Chung, the secretary of the Chinese team at Japan. "We have also extended the invitation for the sake of promoting friendship between the peoples of China and the United States." This was a great surprise. Few people from the West had been able to enter China since the Communist Revolution of 1949. For two decades the Chinese had struggled with internal economic, political, and cultural problems; outsiders were unwelcome. In addition, the American team was not very good compared to teams from the Far East. The Chinese players had placed first in four of six categories; the Americans were far down the line. There was not much that the Chinese could learn from the Americans about the sport.

Table tennis was a recreational game invented in the 1890s by British military officers who batted a small ball across a line of books on a table with small racquets. The first balls were carved from champagne corks. The game was promoted in the early 20th century by the Parker Brothers company as Ping Pong—the name came from the sound of the ball as it alternately hit the table, "ping," and the hollow vellum racquet, "pong." Sandpaper-covered paddles and celluloid balls improved the equipment in the early 20th century. Paddles covered with sponge rubber in the 1950s allowed players to hit the ball with more speed and spin. The game became widely popular in the West as a recreational game, and much less so as a competitive sport.

In China, Japan, the Philippines, and elsewhere in the Far East, however, table tennis became a favorite for both purposes. It spread through the YMCA network and a Shanghai Ping Pong Union formed in 1923. The first international tournament in 1926 was sponsored by the International Table Tennis Federation, which began the same year. In the villages of China there were even cast concrete tables with a concrete ridge used as a net. In 1961, the Chinese hosted a world championship and dominated the game from that time onward.

American Jim Thorpe stole the show in the 1912 Olympic games in Stockholm, Sweden. He won the pentathlon and decathlon, though his medals were later revoked when it was discovered that he had played semiprofessional baseball.

The American captain was thus surprised at the Chinese invitation. With permission from the U.S. State Department, 15 Americans, including 7 men and 2 women players, immediately went to China for eight days. The team traveled to Shanghai and Beijing to give demonstrations and were treated with great cordiality. They were greeted by the Chinese premier, Chou En Lai, who spoke to them about starting a new page of friendly relationships with the United States. The change in attitude coincided with a move to receive China into the United Nations. The American secretary of state, Henry Kissinger, flew secretly to Beijing, the Chinese capital, to make arrangements, and six months later, in 1972 President Richard M. Nixon made a formal visit. In this instance, a very minor sport for the West was used as a goodwill gesture by China to make a very great change in international politics. This process eventually became known as "Ping-Pong Diplomacy."

Sports have long been recognized by politicians as a bridge between peoples. The activity by itself can be politically neutral, and everyone can admire the skill of an accomplished athlete. It is exciting, moreover, for athletes to represent their country and test their skills against foreigners. It can be argued that such international competition tends to decrease fear of others and thus help create tolerance. It is better to compete on the playing field than on the battlefield. Consequently, international competition has become a part of modern sports. The *America*'s Cup in sailing, the Davis Cup for tennis, and the World Cup for soccer are examples. The most important event of global athletics that embraces a variety of sports, however, has been the modern Olympic games. Within the history of the games can be found concerns about minorities, women, technology, nationalism, amateurism, and political conflict. These are many of the same concerns that affect the larger world outside the realm of sport.

The modern Olympic games began as the dream of Baron Pierre de Coubertin (1863–1937). He grew up in Paris, the son of an aristocratic family, at a difficult time for the French. Napoleon III of France failed to establish the Archduke Maximilian on a throne while meddling in Mexican affairs, and worse, lost the Franco-Prussian War of 1870. Paris itself fell under siege during the war and suffered German artillery bombardment. It was a humiliation.

In searching for an explanation of France's losses, the young Coubertin noted the physical fitness of the German soldiers compared to the French. Earlier, in 1810, Friedrich Ludwig Jahn (1778–1852) had built a *turnplatz,* or playground, on the outskirts of Berlin. He taught schoolboys to climb poles, ladders, and ropes to build their physical fitness. The idea spread. It was the beginning of gymnastics, but Jahn saw the exercises as a patriotic effort that built physical fitness as a way to help Germans throw off the rule of the French conqueror, Napoleon I.

Now, Coubertin the Frenchman saw such physical education as a key to German victory. The young baron also believed the English myth that Napoleon I had been defeated at Waterloo in 1815 by English lads trained on the playing fields of Eton. Sports thus might provide a means of recovery from the French defeats. In addition, between 1875 and 1881 German archaeologists uncovered much of the ancient Olympic site in Greece. They found statues, buildings, and 1,300 gold objects. Together, these facts about sport mixed in Coubertin's mind. He traveled widely, including in the United States, talked to sports enthusiasts, and changed his mind about revenge on the Germans. Sports, instead, might be a key to world peace.

Coubertin organized athletics in France, wrote articles about his idea of world games, and personally contacted leaders in Europe and the United States. Representatives from nine nations met at the Sorbonne in Paris in 1894 and agreed with the baron that the Olympic games should be revived and that the first competition should take place in 1896 at Athens. They established the International Olympic Committee (IOC) to make decisions about the games, an organization that continues to the present. With some initial reluctance from the Greeks, the games were held in Athens in a restored U-shaped white marble stadium. About 70,000 spectators and 311 athletes from 13 countries attended (historians are somewhat unsure about the exact numbers).

Most of the fans and 200 of the athletes were Greek. Events in track and field, cycling, fencing, gymnastics, shooting,

swimming, tennis, weightlifting, and wrestling were held. The Greeks won 47 medals, with the United States finishing in second place with 19. The U.S. team was made up of five men from the Boston Athletic Club, four from Princeton, and James B. Connolly, who had to quit school at Harvard in order to compete. Connolly, an Irish American, won the hop-skip-and-jump (triple jump), and became the first athlete to win Olympic honors in 1,500 years. Cheered by noisy sailors on shore leave, the Americans won 9 of the 12 events in track and field.

The most spectacular track event, however, was won by Spiridon Louys, a Greek mailman. A race was held to re-create the feat of Pheidippides, who brought the news of victory to Athens from the battlefield at Marathon in 490 B.C. The distance from Marathon was about 22 miles, and the race ended in the stadium. When the short, spindly Louys entered the arena after running for almost three hours the fans shouted,

On April 6, 1896, at the stadium in Athens, 60,000 people gathered to watch the first modern Olympics. Of the 311 athletes from 13 nations, none was more celebrated than marathon winner Spiridon Louys, a Greek mailman, pictured in traditional dress with other winners.

"Hellene! Hellene!" ("A Greek! A Greek!"). Crown Prince Constantine came out of the stands to accompany Louys to the finish line, and King George of Greece later gave him a horse and wagon for mail delivery, as well as a trophy. The enthusiasm of the Greeks for Louys prompted Charles Maurras, a French writer, to say to Coubertin as they watched the celebration, "I see that your internationalism . . . does not kill national spirit—it strengthens it." It was a warning about the excessive patriotism of the future.

Coubertin was given little credit by the Greeks for his promotion of the Olympics, but the baron remained content, polite, and enthusiastic about the results. The first games were limited to essentials. The swimmers, for example, competed in the Bay of Zea in cold 55 degree water and 12-foot waves. The Olympic games, however, had begun and were held every four years thereafter with the exception of wartime. The ancient tradition of an Olympic peace failed in the modern period. The IOC embraced the concept of amateurism and tried to avoid excessive nationalism. It endorsed committees independent of national governments and switched the location of the games from country to country. In 1920 the Olympics first used as a symbol a flag of five colored rings, and the motto, *Citius, Altius, Fortius*, meaning "Swifter, Higher, Stronger." The torch relay was used first as a part of the opening ceremony at the 1936 Berlin games. The IOC gradually increased the number of events (the winter games were added in 1924), slowly allowed women to compete, and generally supported racial and ethnic equality among competitors.

In 1912, the American team sent to Sweden for the Stockholm games, for example, included Howard P. Drew, an African-American; Duke Kahanamoku, a Hawaiian; and Lewis Tewanima and Jim Thorpe, American Indians. Drew injured himself, Kahanamoku won the 100-meter swim, Tewanima gained second in the 10,000-meter run, and Thorpe won both the pentathlon and decathlon. When King Gustav of Sweden presented Thorpe with his medals, he said, "You, sir, are the greatest athlete in the world." Thorpe replied, "Thanks, King." In 1908 Ralph Rose, the U.S. parade flagbearer at the London games, refused to dip the Stars and Stripes in salute to the British monarch because the English did not fly the U.S. flag with others at the stadium. They said that they could not find one. The refusal to dip the flag in salute became an American tradition after that.

The United States continued to send racially and ethnically mixed teams to the Olympics, and a famous racial incident occurred at the 1936 Berlin games. Under the dictator Adolf Hitler (1889–1945), the Nazis tried to use athletics to advertise the assumed superior qualities of so-called Aryan—white and Nordic—peoples like themselves. They thought other peoples were physically and mentally inferior. They forced Jews out of German sports clubs and looked down upon blacks. This was contrary to the Olympic ideals of equality. When confronted by the president of the IOC, Henri de Baillet-Latour of Belgium, Hitler said, "When you are invited to a friend's home, you don't tell him how to run it, do you?" The IOC president replied,

Jim Thorpe: "The Greatest Athlete in the World"

James F. "Jim" Thorpe (1888–1953) was born in Oklahoma in a one-room cabin. His ancestry was a mix of Sac-Fox Indian, French, and Irish. When he was 16, he began attending the Carlisle Indian School in Pennsylvania, where Coach "Pop" Warner ordered him to run track. Thorpe wanted to play football, however, and Warner tossed him a ball. The coach then instructed the other players to tackle Thorpe to teach him a lesson. With his dazzling speed and strength, however, Thorpe ran over some and left the others "hugging air." Thorpe declared to the coach, "Nobody is going to tackle Jim." From then on Thorpe particpated in football as well as several other sports.

In 1912 Carlisle was considered the best team in the nation. They beat the second-ranked team, Army, by 27-6, with Thorpe carrying the ball and dragging tacklers across the goal line. In 1912, he represented the United States in the Stockholm Olympics, where he won both the pentathlon and decathlon. These events required talent in a variety of track and field skills, and were considered the highest test for an all-around athlete. Unfortunately, the next year a reporter discovered that Thorpe had played semiprofessional baseball in the summer for $15 per week. Technically, this meant that Thorpe was not an amateur athlete. Thorpe admitted it was true, and the Olympic medals were taken from him. After shifts in attitude about amateurism, the International Olympic Committee voted to present replica medals to his daughter in 1983.

From 1913 to 1919 Thorpe played professional baseball for the New York Giants, Cincinnati Reds, and Boston Braves. He also played professional football for various teams, including the Canton Bulldogs and the New York Giants from 1915 to 1928. Because of his fame, Thorpe was elected president of the new National Football League in 1920. He ended his career as a Hollywood stuntman.

Jim Thorpe is greeted by Mayor William Jay Gaynor (third from left) and other dignitaries at New York City's City Hall in recognition of victories in the 1912 games.

"Excuse me, Mr. Chancellor, when the five rings are raised over the stadium, it is no longer Germany. It is the Olympics and we are masters there." German officials assured the IOC and Avery Brundage (1887–1975), president of the American Olympic Association, that there would be no trouble. Brundage, in turn, stopped a boycott of the games led by American Jews, Roman Catholics, and blacks. The U.S. sent teams to both the winter and summer Olympics in Germany.

At Berlin, Hitler pronounced the opening of the games and a recorded message from Baron Coubertin instructed the pro-Nazi crowd: "The important thing at the Olympic Games is not to win, but to take part, just as the important thing about life is not to conquer, but to struggle well." Although German athletes won more medals—89—in the summer games than their American counterparts, who took 56, Aryan supremacy was challenged by the sparkling performances of America's black runners and Korea's Sohn Kee Chung, who won the marathon.

Korea was then under the repressive control of Japan, and Sohn had to run wearing Japanese colors. He had grown up running for pleasure along the Yalu River with rubber soles tied on his feet with a rope. Korean custom dictated slow, dignified walking, but Sohn loved to run. At Berlin he paced himself well in the race and broke the Olympic record by two minutes. In the program he was listed as "Kitei Son," a Japanese translation of his name. On the victory stand, as the Japanese flag was raised in victory and the band played the Japanese national anthem, Sohn, the first Korean champion, lowered his head and wept for his lost country.

It was not an entirely happy occasion for American blacks, either. Hitler had been making a show of congratulating the German winners. The IOC asked him to stop and he did. He left the stadium shortly before the awards ceremony for Cornelius

Johnson and David Albritton, American blacks who had placed first and second in the high jump. The sequence of events has sometimes been interpreted as a "snub" by Hitler, but he had already stopped his greetings. It made little difference, however. Earlier, he had said in propaganda sheets, "The Americans ought to be ashamed of themselves for letting their medals be won by Negroes. I myself would never shake hands with one of them."

*Sohn Kee Chung rounds a
bend on his way to winning
the the Olympic marathon
in 1936. Although a native
of Korea, he was forced to
participate under the flag of
Japan, which ruled Korea at
the time.*

The great African-American hero of the games was James C. "Jesse" Owens (1918–80). Born in Alabama, he revealed early an effortless, efficient running style. He attended Ohio State University and in one afternoon in 1935 set three world records and tied a fourth. At the Berlin Olympics he won four gold medals—100- and 200-meter sprints, long jump, and 400-meter relay. During the long-jump competition, he developed a friendship with Luz Long, the German who came in second. After Owens's victory, the blond Long walked arm-in-arm with Owens around the stadium to the discomfort of Nazi fans. Later, Long died fighting for Germany in Sicily during World War II. Owens afterward became an inspirational speaker and product advertiser in America, a land in which racial segregation was still a part of daily life. "I wasn't invited to shake hands with Hitler," Owens later commented, "but I wasn't invited to the White House to shake hands with the President, either."

The United States' difficulty with race surfaced again at the Mexico City Olympics in 1968. The IOC was not the problem. It had banned from competition the Union of South Africa for its apartheid, or segregationist, policies. Harry Edwards, a sociologist in California, and others thought that a boycott by African-Americans would draw attention to racial distress within the nation. The attempted boycott failed. At a victory ceremony for the 200-meter sprint, however, Tommie Smith, who won first, and John Carlos, who placed third, mounted the stand, bowed their heads during the national anthem, and raised a fist covered with a black glove in a "black power"

salute. The embarrassed United States Olympic Committee (USOC) sent the two black athletes home the following day. On the last day of track competition, the winning U.S. 1,600-meter relay team did the same thing.

These gestures, which reflected troubles within the United States, overshadowed the athletic achievements. Al Oerter of New York won his fourth and final consecutive discus championship; Bob Beamon of New York shattered the long-jump record by almost two feet; Dick Fosbury from Portland demonstrated his backward "flop," which revolutionized high jumping; George Foreman from Houston won the heavyweight division of boxing and pranced around the ring carrying a small American flag; and African runners led by Kip Keino Kipchoge of Kenya won almost all of the distance events.

The Mexico City Olympics was also noteworthy because they were the only summer games since 1952 at which United States athletes won more medals than those from the Soviet Union (107-91). Following World War II, the USSR used the Olympic games to compete peacefully with the United States. From 1945 until 1993, the United States and USSR were locked into a cold war that affected politics, economics, and military matters. Each nation tried to prove its superiority by supporting large armies, building complex war machines, and attempting to influence foreign peoples with loans of money and exported technology. Culture and sports were also involved.

The reasoning—somewhat illogical—of Cold War athletics was that the better country would produce the best athletes. The world, therefore, would applaud and support the democracy of the United States, or the communism of the Soviet Union as a response. The Olympic games thus became a forum for Cold War competition. Perhaps, it was a fortunate development—American and Soviet troops never shot at

Tommie Smith (center) and John Carlos (right) took the winners' stand without shoes and gave the Black Power salute to protest racism in the U.S. The track and field stars were rushed home by an embarrassed U.S. government.

Emil Zatopek: An Unlikely Champion

At Helsinki in 1952, the stadium crowd chanted "Za-to-pek! Za-to-pek! Za-to-pek!" as an unlikely champion set records in the 5,000 meters, 10,000 meters, and marathon runs. He was scrawny, partly bald, and ran looking like he might collapse at any moment. His head rolled from side to side, his face turned red, his tongue hung out, his arms flailed the air. The crowd loved him.

Born in 1922 in Czechoslovakia and the son of a laborer, Zatopek was fast enough to attract special attention from his government. He joined the army so that he could run. Using a flashlight and wearing army boots, he trained at night and developed a new method of conditioning. He ran repeated high-speed, 100-yard sprints interspersed with slow jogs. It became known as interval training. He was inexhaustible and won the marathon at the 1952 Olympic games although he had never run one before.

In 1968, when the Soviet Union invaded Czechoslovakia with its tanks to suppress a liberal communist government, the Olympic champion protested. He argued that communism had to give people "air to breathe." As a result of his patriotism, Zatopek was stripped of his army rank, thrown out of the Communist party, and had to work 10 to 14 hours per day at hard manual labor in order to live. Eventually, he obtained a job translating foreign sports journals at the Ministry of Sport. The government, however, refused to allow him to travel and the world lost sight of Zatopek for 22 years. In 1990, with the end of the cold war, the Czechoslovakian government apologized and restored Zatopek's lost army rank.

Emil "The Flying Czech" Zatopek of Czechoslovakia nears the finish line of a five-mile race in São Paulo, Brazil, in 1954.

one another in a war. It may be that athletic competition helped to promote understanding and reduce tension between the two countries.

The Soviets sent observers to the 1948 games in London and appeared with full teams in 1952 at Helsinki. There, the United States won 76 medals and the USSR took 69. Thereafter, only in the 1968 Mexico summer games did the United States win more medals. The Soviets were not burdened with the concept of amateurism. They identified their athletes at a young age, sent them for coaching at special schools, provided jobs for them that allowed plenty of time for training, secretly gave them cash rewards when they won, and made them national heroes. The Soviet public preferred to watch soccer, ice hockey, and basketball, but the government also paid attention to the less popular Olympic sports in order to win medals.

The goal was to win, and in the climate of the cold war, nations did not hesitate to cheat. In 1957, Herman Ratgent, a German athlete, said that the Nazis forced him to compete as a woman in 1936. This added fuel to the rumors about men posing as women. Consequently, at the 1966 Bucharest track championships the women were forced to undergo physical exams by doctors to ascertain that the athletes were really women. Chromosomal evaluation of cells scraped from inside the cheek later replaced the physical examination. This has been interpreted by women athletes as an irritating challenge not only to their honesty, but also to their femininity.

Worse, the IOC slowly recognized that drugs unjustly could make someone a bet-

In 1976, the German Democratic Republic took a gold medal in the womens 400-meter relay and set a new world record of 4:07.95 in doing it. Pictured here are Ulrike Richter, Hannelore Anke, Andrea Pollack, and Kornelia Ender.

ter athlete. Officials began testing in 1967, but it took some time before their testing procedure was effective. Husky female swimmers from East Germany dominated the events at the 1976 Montreal games. They won 11 of 13 races, and when Shirley Babashoff, a U.S. sprinter, suggested that their unusual deep voices came from using male hormones, an official for the East German team quipped, "They came to swim, not to sing." Their use of anabolic steroids, synthetic hormones that promote muscle growth to give them strength, was later confirmed. The East Germans also experimented with pumping air into the intestines of swimmers so that they could float better. This experiment was painful and did not work.

Athletes from the United States were also involved in the cheating. Drug experimentation among weight lifters in York, Pennsylvania, began in the early 1950s. The use of dianabol, a steroid that would increase muscle mass and strength, was in common use among American and Soviet athletes in the 1960s. At the 1983 Pan American games, tests found banned performance-enhancing drugs in the blood of 15 athletes from 10 nations, all of whom had to return their medals. Twelve U.S. track and field athletes hurriedly returned home rather than submit to the tests.

In 1984 U.S. bikers used blood transfusions to increase their capacity to use oxygen. "Blood doping," as this practice is called, was legal at the time. At the 1988 Seoul Olympics, Canadian sprinter Ben Johnson, who won the 100-meter race, was sent home in disgrace for drug use. Some Canadian weight lifters, moreover, tried

to avoid detection of steroids by injecting "clean" urine into their bladders through a tube up their penises. In 1993–94, 13 record-breaking Chinese female swimmers were caught using a steroid drug and banned from competition. Because of the desire to win at all costs, the drug problem has become pervasive throughout the Olympic and athletic world.

The cold war also led to a U.S. refusal to attend the summer Olympic games of 1980 held in Moscow. The boycott took place at the request of President Jimmy Carter because of the USSR invasion of Afghanistan. Sixty-two nations followed the U.S. lead; eighty-one nations attended. The boycott did not stop the war in Afghanistan, and it was the deprived athletes who were hurt the most by the boycott. In 1984, when the summer games took place in Los Angeles, the Soviets and 13 communist nations retaliated against the 1980 U.S. boycott by refusing to attend the games there. One noticeable outcome of the 1984 games, however, was that American women such as Mary Lou Retton in gymnastics and Joan Benoit in running became superstars.

Women were first allowed to compete at the Paris games of 1900. Margaret Abbott of Chicago, who was studying art in the French capital, took time off to win a gold medal in golf. Her championship was more of a coincidence than anything else, the

Canada's Ben Johnson set a world record in the 100-meter dash in 1988. Three days later, he was stripped of his Olympic medal after testing positive for performance-enhancing drugs.

result of an upper-class upbringing. Golf, along with tennis, was later dropped from the Olympic schedule. Archery was added in 1904, and tennis reinstated for women in 1908. Figure skating for men and women came in 1908 and swimming for women in 1912. Support for women's events conflicted with the prejudice against female sports in the first half of the 20th century. Diver Aileen Riggin recalled about 1920:

In those days women did not compete in strenuous athletics. No one swam very far. It was not considered healthy for girls to overexert themselves or to swim as far as a mile. People thought it was a great mistake, that we were ruining our health, that we would never have children, and that we would be sorry for it later on. There was a great deal of publicity against women competing in athletics at all. We had to combat this feeling at every turn.

There were exceptions, however, such as Riggin, Gertrude Ederle, and the remarkable "Babe" Didrikson. Born of

"Babe" Didrikson: "Muscle Moll"

In 1932 she was 5 feet 7 inches tall and weighed 128 pounds. She had green eyes, sandy-colored hair, a thin build, and was the best female American athlete of the first half of the 20th century. She was a natural athlete who found her life in the competition of sports. A tomboy who wore overalls to parties, she said rather sadly, "I know I'm not pretty, but I do try to be graceful."

Didrikson dropped out of school to play basketball for the Employer's Casualty Company of Dallas in a business athletic league. At the urging of the company, she began to participate in track and field as well. She won six gold medals at the 1932 AAU track meet, which qualified her to compete in the Los Angeles

Olympic games that same year. At Los Angeles she won the javelin and 80-meter hurdles. She took first in the high jump too, but the judges changed it to second place because she went over the bar head first, which was considered incorrect form. Her irritated teammates were happy she got second because "Babe" was also loud, obnoxious, self-centered, and a braggart. When no one paid attention to her, she would loudly play a harmonica in order to interrupt conversations.

As a result of her Olympic victories, however, she drew the attention of the national newspapers as a sports hero. She learned to deal with intrusive questions, to handle a world that disparaged women

athletes as "Muscle Molls," and to curb her brash behavior. Didrikson played both amateur and professional golf for 20 years after 1935, and married professional wrestler George Zaharias in 1938. She was impressed with George, she claimed, because he was the only man she had ever met who could hit a golf ball farther than she could.

She continued on the professional tour until 1955, a much admired player and person. In 1956, Didrickson died of cancer.

The biggest star of the 1932 Olympics in Los Angeles was Mildred "Babe" Didrickson. She won the javelin and 80-meter hurdles, and placed second in the high jump.

Norwegian immigrants in Port Arthur, Texas, Mildred Ella Didrikson (1911–56) grew up in Beaumont, Texas. She was called "Babe" by her schoolmates because she hit home runs like "Babe" Ruth in sandlot baseball games. She loved sports and was disappointed that she was not allowed to play high school football. She dropped out of school, played basketball on a female team in Dallas, and entered the 1932 AAU track meet in preparation for the Los Angeles Olympics. In one afternoon, she won six gold medals, set four world records, and won the team championship by herself. At Los Angeles she broke the javelin record by 11 feet, won the 80-meter hurdles in record time, and took second in high jump. She became a national hero. Afterward, Didrikson took up golf and played mainly as a professional.

Like Ederle and other women athletes of her time, however, Didrikson was an exception. It was not fashionable for women to be athletic. Babe was not a crusader like Billie Jean King; she just loved sports. The cold war and the Olympics, however, changed attitudes and opened a door of opportunity for women athletes. In 1952 there were only 9 track and field events for women, and 24 for men. The United States took only 10 women to Helsinki on its Olympic team that year. The Soviet Union, however, exploited the lack of participation by Western women, and much of their success in cold war Olympic competition came from their use of female athletes.

The United States government, particularly the State Department, grew concerned about the Olympic success of the USSR. It urged the USOC to do something to encourage American women. In 1960 Doris Duke Cromwell, the wealthy heiress of the Duke tobacco fortune, gave $500,000 to the USOC—then a poor agency—to investigate ways to improve female performance. The push from the Olympics coincided with the feminist movement within the United States. Television portrayals of fine female athletes from the Olympics (Mary Lou Retton, Jackie Joyner-Kersee, and Joan Benoit, to name only a few) and elsewhere eventually changed attitudes. Ideals of beauty changed, female muscles became acceptable. It became all right for women to be strong, to be athletes. In 1992 at the Barcelona games there were still 24 track and field events for men as there had been in 1952. But now, instead of 9 as in 1952, there were 19 for women. There was also comparable expansion in other Olympic sports. It was not quite equality—in 1996 at Atlanta there were 6,582 male and 3,779 female Olympians—but during the 100 years of the modern Olympics there has been considerable progress for women.

The cold war not only helped women's athletics, it also destroyed the old concept of amateurism. When the Soviet Union began to send state-supported athletes to the Olympics in 1952, the IOC refused to take sides. This meant that countries such as Canada, the United States, and Great Britain were left on their own with long-standing ideals of amateur competition. In the United States, the pressures of cold war athletic losses gradually wore down the principle that only a person who was not paid could compete. It was galling, for example, to lose

Nadia Comaneci: A Perfect Ten

In 1972, the 17-year-old Olga Korbut of the Soviet Union used her pigtails, daring back somersaults on the uneven bars, and smiling personality to make the world aware of gymnastics. With the attention of the world focused on Korbut's return in 1976 to the Montreal Olympics, few paid attention to a grim 14-year-old girl from Romania, Nadia Comaneci. Trained by Bela Karolyi, who discovered her pretending to be a gymnast in a schoolyard, Comaneci's life became mats, balance beams, and uneven bars. She was 4 feet 11 inches tall, weighed 86 pounds, and was shy. Comaneci, however, possessed a cold, competitive drive. "When the coach was telling me to do 10, I do 20," she said later. "I was always doing extra. I liked it when something was very, very hard to do." She whizzed flawlessly through her Olympic routines and scored seven perfect "10s" on her way to three gold medals. No one in the world had ever scored seven perfect "10s." She never smiled, however, even during the warm applause of the spectators.

Interest in gymnastics, a minor sport, derived from exercise routines in Germany, boomed in America following the performances of Korbut and Comaneci. Korbut gained weight, married, had a child, and drifted away from gymnastics. Comaneci had a "nervous breakdown," recovered, won a gold medal on the balance beam at the 1980 Moscow Olympics, and

fled to New York in 1989. She escaped the collapse of communism in Romania and the Soviet Union. Bela Karolyi, her coach, also escaped to the West and set up training quarters in Houston, Texas. Mary Lou Retton, a star of the 1984 Los Angeles games, was one of his U.S. pupils.

At various gymnastics competitions, Comaneci had met Bart Conner, who won two gold medals at the Los Angeles Olympics in 1984. In 1990, Conner, who worked as a sports commentator in Oklahoma, made an effort to see her again on a television show in Los Angeles. Telephone calls and meetings resulted in friendship and

finally marriage in 1996. Comaneci continued to train, and her coach Paul Ziert in Oklahoma, commented, "The first time I worked with her, she always did her job very well . . . but I also noticed how closed she was, how uncomfortable she was in public. She let you see very little inside because that's how she learned to be in Romania." In time, she changed. "She's just blossomed into the most lovely rose you've ever seen," said Ziert. Bart Conner commented at the reopening of the International Gymnastics Hall of Fame in Norman, Oklahoma, in 1997, "Most guys brag that their wives are a ten. My wife is *the* ten."

In an imperfect Games beset by boycotts and high costs, Romanian gymnast Nadia Comaneci, 14, was perfection. She earned the first score of 10 in the history of the sport.

51-50 in the championship round of basketball, America's own home-grown sport, to the Soviets in 1972. The contest was protested due to last-second inbound passes, and the United States refused the second-place silver medals. It was easy for U.S. fans to grumble that this could never happen if American professional players were allowed to compete. That, of course, happened in 1992 when the so-called Dream Team of National Basketball Association professionals easily won the gold medal at Barcelona.

Amateurism basically ended in America with the passage of the Amateur Sports Act of 1978. A three-cornered fight between the United States Olympic Committee, Amateur Athletic Union, and National Collegiate Athletic Association over the control of athletes and competition had created frustrations in fielding international teams in 1972 and 1976. Particularly bitter was the fight between the AAU, which often sanctioned international competition, and the NCAA, which controlled college sports. The two organizations would ban each other's athletes from competition, and sometimes individual athletes were members of both groups. The athletes, thus, were caught in the middle of the fight and U.S. international teams suffered. Attempts at mediation repeatedly failed until Congress passed the Amateur Sports Act, which essentially put the USOC in control as the coordinating body for all Olympic sports. Each sport was ruled by it own national governing body, such as U.S. Swimming, Inc., for all swimmers in the country.

These governing bodies determined eligibility, sponsored meets, selected Olympic athletes, and held workshops for coaches.

They were supported by the USOC with funds and training centers. They were also allowed to set up trust funds for athletes based on prizes at meets and other earnings connected with the sport. The athlete could then draw on the fund for training expenses. A House of Delegates made up of representatives from the governing bodies and the NCAA set the policies for the USOC.

Although there were differences between governing bodies about eligibility, the old ideas of amateurism fell. The change allowed professional tennis stars to compete at the Seoul games in 1988, where Pam Shriver and Zina Garrison of the United States won women's doubles, and enabled the Dream Team to play basketball at Barcelona in 1992, and again in Atlanta in 1996. The USOC thus became the most important sports organization in the United States.

The reorganization made it possible for the United States to compete more effectively with the Soviet Union. Olympic sports received not only recognition and money, but also better training information. The USOC sponsored training centers for scientific research about athletics. Runners were put on treadmills, swimmers in flumes, archers on high-speed film in order to figure out the best techniques. In this respect, the scientific revolution of Western civilization was applied in a systematic way to U.S. sports.

The cold war ended with the fall of the Berlin Wall in 1989 and the subsequent breakup of the USSR. The Soviet Sports Ministry shut down in January 1992. A United Team of countries from the former

USSR, nonetheless, competed in the 1992 Barcelona Olympics and gathered more medals than the United States. It remains to be seen how international political rivalry will be expressed in the Olympic games in the future. Although the great competition between the United States and USSR ended, it is likely that political conflicts will continue to be expressed on the scene of international competition. The Finns objected to conquest by the Russians in 1912; the Hungarian-Soviet water polo match left blood in the water in 1956 after the brutal suppression of the Hungarian Revolution; and 29 African nations boycotted the 1976 Montreal Olympics because of segregation in the Union of South Africa.

The worst incident of political conflict, however, occurred at the Munich games in 1972. Palestinian terrorists penetrated the Olympic village and took hostage nine Israeli athletes on September 5. This was a part of the ongoing warfare and hostility between Israel, a Jewish state, and its Arab

On September 5, 1972, eight Palestinian terrorists took eleven Israeli Olympians hostage. The hostages, five terrorists, and one policeman died, and many people called for the Games to end.

Mark Spitz: A Porpoise In and Out of the Water

As a brash, pampered 18-year-old swimmer from California, Mark Spitz bragged that he would win six gold medals at the Mexico Olympics in 1968. Disliked and ignored by his teammates, Spitz lived in a room by himself and took only two gold medals, both in relays, which are team, not individual, events. Somewhat more mature, and admired for his talent and hard work, Spitz returned to Olympic competition in 1972 in Munich. In the most astonishing feat in Olympic history, Spitz won seven events, all of them in world record time—100- and 200-meter freestyle, 100- and 200-meter butterfly, and three relays.

Spitz became the first Olympic athlete to sign large post-competition endorsement contracts (worth about $5 million). According to *Sports Illustrated*, a poster of Spitz posed in the team racing suit with the seven gold medals around his neck became the most popular selling photograph of any athlete at the time. He was signed for commercials and movies, but all faltered. "I was a porpoise out of water," he said. "All my life I had done little except concentrate on my swimming. I was determined to be the best in the world. I never learned how to relate to my friends and the public." Spitz became a motivational speaker, a real-estate investor, and promoter of Swatch watches. A well-publicized attempt to regain his earlier success for the 1992 Olympic games faded when he failed to swim fast enough to make the team.

The first ten days of the 1972 Munich Olympics belonged to Mark Spitz, who won seven gold medals in swimming events.

neighbors. Twenty-three hours later, the terrorists tried to escape with their hostages and confronted the German police in a shootout at the airport. All the hostages, five Palestinians, and one policeman were killed. The games, the first on German soil since 1936, continued in spite of this. Mark Spitz, an American Jew, won seven gold medals and set seven Olympic records. News of the kidnapping broke as Spitz prepared for a press conference after his final triumph. He was surrounded by American swimming officials at the interview, and then flown to England for safety. Political disagreements projected onto Olympic competition will likely continue. Yet there is something important about the interest of nations and people in the global competition that the games offer. In 1896 an estimated 311 athletes from 13 nations took part in the Olympics; in 1996 there were 11,000 athletes from 197 nations. Wealthy professional athletes were willing to compete and risk injury for the sake of an Olympic medal. It was a chance to prove that they were the best in the world.

But the competition means more than that. During the sailing races at the Seoul Olympics in 1988, Canadian Laurence Lemieux gave up his own chances to win a medal in order to save the life of a competitor from Singapore. The man's boat had capsized and the injured sailor was drowning in the water 25 meters from his overturned boat. Lemieux left the course, sailed close by, and took his fellow competitor on board. Lemieux's position in the competition slipped from 2nd to a hopeless 21st. Lemieux, however, was willing to lose in order to do what was right. A jury, recognizing the circumstances, allowed the Canadian to continue the sailing competition as if he were in second place. The judges were also right. This story illustrates what sports can mean in the best of circumstances.

Athletic competition provides a stage to demonstrate the highest qualities of human character. International competition allows for a transcendence beyond national interests and regions to touch the common core of humanity.

Laurence Lemieux of Canada provided an example of sportsmanship for all athletes when he dropped out of second place to help a fellow athlete from Singapore who was drowning because his boat had tipped over. Lemieux is pictured here just after that memorable race in the 1988 Seoul Olympics.

Epilogue

The people of the modern world have an abiding, passionate interest in sports. Athletic events recorded in the newspaper, broadcast by television, or performed in arenas provide a topic of conversation and analysis. Everyone becomes an expert and has an opinion. Sports permeate out lives and provide everyone something to talk or write about. Sports thus give cohesion to society and act as a kind of "glue." Sports activities create a common interest that helps to hold a school, city, or nation together.

Sports are also an integral part, not a separate part, of human life. They have been so from the beginning of human existence. To some extent, we are all spectators and participants. Sports have been not only reflective of great human struggles, such as the worldwide efforts to gain civil and human rights, and the shattering of gender and racial barriers, but also vitally involved in these human dramas. Perhaps, with the end of the Cold War, the intense nationalism often associated with sports will recede. We might learn to cheer an Olympic champion, or World Cup victor, as a representative of all humanity. It would make no difference the color, politics, religion, gender, or origin of the participants. We could still have our heroes and favorite teams, of course—that is part of the fun—but there would be a prevailing recognition that sports competition celebrates the athlete in all of us.

Chronology

B.C.

2300

Wrestling boys portrayed on tomb walls at Saqquara, Egypt

2300

Wrestling match recorded in the *Epic of Gilgamesh*

776

Beginning of the ancient Olympic Games

700

The Iliad records the funeral games of Patroclus

536-516

Milo of Kroton wins six wrestling championships in the Ancient Olympics

490

Pheidippides runs from Marathon to Athens

264

First gladiator contests in Rome

200

Mesoamerican ball games

23

First Sumo wrestling

A.D.

72-82

Roman Colosseum built

c. 500

Unarmed martial arts begin in China

1249

Sixty Knights killed in a tournament near Cologne

1275

Kublai Khan and court compete with falcons

1636

Jesuit missionaries observe lacrosse in North America

1754

Royal and Ancient Golf Club of St. Andrews established

1766

Tattersalls market for race horses opens in London

1787

Marylebone Cricket Club established in London

1810

Tom Cribb defeats Tom Molyneaux in boxing

1845

Knickerbocker Base Ball Club plays its first game

1855

First hockey game played in Canada

1857

America's Cup yacht races established

1863

Football Association of London writes rules for soccer

1876

National League forms for baseball

1880's

Walter Camp forms the rules for football

1882

Jigaro Kano starts a school for judo in Japan

1888

First professional rodeo at Prescott, Arizona

1891

James Naismith invents basketball

1892

John L. Sullivan loses to "Gentleman Jim" Corbett in boxing

1893

First Stanley Cup for hockey won by Montreal Amateur Athletic Association

1896

First modern Olympic Games

1899

American League begins to compete in baseball

1900

United States beats England in the first Davis Cup tennis competition

1903

Maurice Garin wins the first Tour de France bicycle race

1903

Boston beats Philadelphia in the first baseball world series

1911

Ray Herroun wins the first Indianapolis 500 auto race

1917

National Hockey League established

1920

National Football League starts as the American Professional Football Association

1926

Gertrude Ederle sets the record for swimming the English Channel

1927

Jack Dempsey loses to Gene Tunney with a "long count" in boxing

1927

"Babe" Ruth hits 60 home runs

1930

First World Cup for soccer won by Uruguay

1930

Bobby Jones wins the "Grand Slam" of golf

1932

"Babe" Didrikson wins one silver and two gold medals in Olympics

1936

"Jesse" Owens wins four gold medals in Olympic track

1938

Joe Louis knocks out Max Schmeling in the first round

1945

First modern Tae Kwon Do school opens in Seoul, Korea

1947

Jackie Robinson breaks the color line in baseball

1949

National Basketball Association forms

1954

Roger Bannister breaks four minutes in the mile run

1959

Vince Lombardi becomes head football coach of the Green Bay Packers

1960

American Football League forms

1961

Rober Maris hits 61 home runs

1961

Wide World of Sports begins broadcasts

1965

Houston Astrodome opens

1967

First Super Bowl of football won by the Green Bay Packers

1967

Muhammad Ali refuses induction into the U.S. Army

1967

Olympic officials begin drug testing

1968

Tommie Smith and John Carlos give a black power salute at the Mexico Olympics

1970

Monday night football broadcasts begin

1972

Mark Spitz wins seven gold medals in Olympic swimming

1972

Title IX becomes law

1973

Billie Jean King beats Bobby Riggs in the "Battle of the Sexes"

1973

Secretariat wins the Triple Crown of horse racing

1976

Nadia Comaneci awarded seven perfect scores in Olympic gymnastics

1984

Joan Benoit wins the first Olympic women's marathon

1986

Jack Nicklaus wins his sixth Masters golf tournament

1997

Tiger Woods wins the Masters golf tournament by 12 strokes

1997

Women's National Basketball Association begins its first season

1998

United States wins first women's Olympic hockey championship

Further Reading

General

Arlott, J., ed. *Oxford Companion to Sports and Games*. Oxford: Oxford University Press, 1976.

Baker, William J. *Sports in the Western World*. Urbana: University of Illinois Press, 1988.

Bannister, Roger. *First Four Minutes*. London: Sportsmans Book Club, 1956.

Benoit, Joan, with Sally Baker. *Running Tide*. New York: Knopf, 1987.

Diagram Group. *Rules of the Game*. Rev. ed. New York: St. Martin's, 1995.

Gorn, Elliott J., and Warren Goldstein. *A Brief History of American Sports*. New York: Hill and Wang, 1993.

Guttmann, Allen. *From Ritual to Record: The Nature of Modern Sports*. New York: Columbia University Press, 1978.

———. *Sports Spectators*. New York: Columbia University Press, 1986.

———. *Women's Sports: A History*. New York: Columbia University Press, 1991.

———. *Games and Empires: Modern Sports and Cultural Imperialism*. New York: Columbia University Press, 1994.

Holt, Richard. *Sport and Society in Modern France*. London: Macmillan, 1981.

Howell, Nancy, and Maxwell L. Howell. *Sports and Games in Canadian Life*. Toronto: Macmillan, 1969.

Johnson, William, ed. *Sport and Physical Education around the World*. Champaign, Ill.: Stipes, 1980.

Levinson, David, and Karen Christensen, eds. *The Encyclopedia of World Sport*. Santa Barbara, Calif.: ABC-CLIO, 1996.

Lowe, Benjamin. *The Beauty of Sport: A Cross-Disciplinary Inquiry*. Englewood Cliffs, N.J.: Prentice-Hall, 1977.

Lucas, John A., and Ronald A. Smith. *Saga of American Sport*. Philadelphia: Lea & Febiger, 1978.

Menke, Frank G. *The Encyclopedia of Sports*. 4th revised ed. New York: A. S. Barnes, 1969.

Novak, Michael. *The Joy of Sports: End Zones, Bases, Baskets, Balls, and the Consecration of the American Spirit*. New York: Basic Books, 1976.

Rader, Benjamin G. *American Sports: From the Age of Folk Games to the Age of Televised Sports*. 3d ed. Englewood Cliffs, N.J.: Prentice Hall, 1996.

Russell, Bill, and Taylor Branch. *Second Wind: The Memoirs of an Opinionated Man*. New York: Ballantine, 1979.

Trengove, Alan. *The Story of the Davis Cup*. London: Stanley Paul, 1985.

Vamplew, Wray. *The Turf: A Social and Economic History of Horse Racing*. London: Allen Lane, 1976.

Van Dalen, Deobold B., and Bruce L. Bennett. *A World History of Physical Education: Cultural, Philosophical, Comparative*. 2d ed. Englewood Cliffs, N.J.: Prentice-Hall, 1971.

Wagner, Eric A., ed. *Sport in Asia and Africa*. Westport, Conn.: Greenwood Press, 1989.

Wright, Graeme. *Rand McNally Illustrated Dictionary of Sports*. Chicago: Rand McNally, 1978.

Zeigler, Earle F., ed. *A History of Sport and Physical Education to 1900*. Champaign, Ill.: Stipes, 1973.

Traditional Sports and Early Civilizations

Baker, William J., and James A. Mangan, eds. *Sport in Africa: Essays in Social History*. New York: Africana Publishing, 1987.

Brasch, R. *How Did Sports Begin? A Look at the Origins of Man at Play*. New York: McKay, 1970.

Cuyler, P. L. *Sumo: From Rite to Sport*. New York: Weatherhill, 1979.

Decker, Wolfgang. *Sports and Games of Ancient Egypt*. Translated by Allen Guttmann. New Haven, Conn.: Yale University Press, 1992.

The Epic of Gilgamesh. Translated by Sumaya Shabandar. Berkshire, England: Garnet, 1994.

Henderson, Robert W. *Ball, Bat, and Bishop: The Origin of Ball Games*. New York: Rockport, 1947.

Olivova, Vera. *Sports and Games in the Ancient World*. New York: St. Martin's, 1984.

Salzman, Mark. *Iron and Silk*. New York: Vintage, 1986.

Stern, Theodore. *The Rubber Ball-Games of the Americas.* Seattle: University of Washington Press, 1949.

Weyand, A. M., and M. R. Roberts. *The Lacrosse Story.* Baltimore, Md.: Herman, 1965.

Greek and Roman Athletics

Cameron, Alan. *Circus Factions: Blues and Greens at Rome and Byzantium.* Oxford: Clarendon, 1976.

Gardiner, E. Norman. *Athletics of the Ancient World.* London: Oxford University Press, 1930.

Homer. *The Iliad.* Translated by E. V. Rieu. Middlesex, England: Penguin, 1950.

———. *The Odyssey of Homer.* Traslated by Allen Mandelbaum. Berkeley: University of California, 1990.

Miller, Stephen G., ed. *Arete: Greek Sports from Ancient Sources.* Berkeley: University of California Press, 1991.

Roland, Auguet. *Cruelty and Civilization: The Roman Games.* London: George Allen and Unwin, 1972.

Swaddling, Judith. *The Ancient Olympic Games.* Austin: University of Texas Press, 1980.

Sweet, Waldo E., ed. *Sport and Recreation in Ancient Greece.* New York: Oxford University Press, 1987.

Sports in Early Western Civilization

Adelman, Melvin L. *A Sporting Time.* Urbana: University of Illinois Press, 1986.

Brailsford, Dennis. *Sport and Society: Elizabeth to Anne.* London: Routledge & Kegan Paul, 1969.

Cripps-Day, Francis Henry. *The History of the Tournament in England and France.* London: Bernard Quartich, 1918.

de Luze, Albert. *A History of the Royal Game of Tennis.* Translated by Sir Richard Hamilton. Kineton: Roundwood, 1979.

Jarvis, Fred B. *The First Hundred Years: A Portrait of NYAC.* London: Macmillan, 1969.

Hemingway, Ernest. *Death in the Afternoon.* New York: Scribners, 1960.

Marvin, Garry. *Bullfight.* Oxford: Basil Blackwell, 1988.

Mitchell, Timothy. *Blood Sport: A Social History of Spanish Bullfighting.* Philadelphia: University of Pennsylvania Press, 1991.

Phillips-Brit, Douglas. *The History of Yachting.* New York: Stein & Day, 1974.

Riess, Steven A. *City Games.* Urbana: University of Illinois Press, 1989.

Somers, Dale A. *The Rise of Sports in New Orleans, 1850–1900.* Baton Rouge: Louisiana State University Press, 1972.

Sports in Great Britian and Its Empire

Altham, H. S. *A History of Cricket.* London: Allen & Unwin, 1962.

Arantes do Nascimento, Edson (Pelé), and Robert L. Fish. *My Life and the Beautiful Game.* Garden City, N.J.: Doubleday, 1977.

Bowen, Rowland. *Cricket: A History of Its Growth and Development throughout the World.* London: Eyre & Spottiswoode, 1970.

Dunning, Eric, and Kenneth Sheard. *Barbarians, Gentlemen and Players: A Sociological Study of the Development of Rugby Football.* New York: New York University Press, 1979.

Holt, Richard. *Sport and the British: A Modern History.* Oxford: Oxford University Press, 1989.

Mangan, J. A., ed. *The Cultural Bond: Sport, Empire, and Society.* London: Frank Cass, 1992.

Mason, Tony. *Association Football and English Society, 1863–1915.* Atlantic Highlands, N.J.: Humanities Press, 1980.

Walvin, James. *The People's Game: A Social History of British Football.* London: Allen Lane, 1975.

Wilde, Simon. *Ranji.* London: Kingswood Press, 1990.

Sports in the Americas

Alexander, Charles C. *Ty Cobb.* New York: Oxford University Press, 1984.

Allen, E. John B. *From Skisport to Skiing.* Amherst: University of Massachusetts Press, 1993.

Arbena, Joseph L., ed. *Sport and Society in Latin America: Diffusion, Dependency, and the Rise of Mass Culture*. Westport, Conn.: Greenwood Press, 1988.

Ashe, Arthur R., Jr. *Hard Road to Glory: A History of the African-American Athlete*. New York: Warner, 1988.

Baker, William J. *Jesse Owens: An American Life*. New York: Free Press, 1986.

Bale, John, and Joseph Maguire, eds. *The Global Sports Arena*. London: Frank Cass, 1993.

Beezley, William H. *Judas at the Jockey Club*. Lincoln: University of Nebraska Press, 1987.

Bruce, Janet. *The Kansas City Monarchs: Champions of Black Baseball*. Lawrence: University Press of Kansas, 1985.

Creamer, Robert W. *Babe: The Legend Comes to Life*. New York: Simon & Schuster, 1974.

Claasen, Harold. *The History of Professional Football*. Englewood Cliffs, N.J.: Prentice-Hall, 1963.

Dulles, Foster Rhea. *A History of Recreation: America Learns to Play*. 2nd ed. New York: Appleton-Century-Crofts, 1965.

Durso, Joseph. *Madison Square Garden: 100 Years of History*. New York: Simon & Schuster, 1979.

Edelman, Robert. *Serious Fun*. New York: Oxford University Press, 1993.

Edwards, Harry. *The Revolt of the Black Athlete*. New York: Free Press, 1969.

Fredriksson, Kristine. *American Rodeo: From Buffalo Bill to Big Business*. College Station: Texas A&M University Press, 1985.

Gorn, Elliott J. *The Manly Art: Bare-Knuckle Prize Fighting in America*. Ithaca, N.Y.: Cornell University Press, 1986.

Grimsley, Will. *Golf: Its History, People, and Events*. Englewood Cliffs, N.J.: Prentice-Hall, 1966.

Groussard, Serge. *The Blood of Israel*. Translated by Harold J. Salemson. New York: William Morrow, 1975.

Guttmann, Allen. *Sports Spectators*. New York: Columbia University Press, 1986.

Hickok, Ralph. *The Encyclopedia of North American Sports History*. New York: Facts on File, 1992.

Isaacs, Neil. *Checking Back: A History of the National Hockey League*. New York: Norton, 1977.

Johnson, Elmer L. *The History of YMCA Physical Education*. Chicago: Follett, 1979.

Johnson, William Oscar, and Nancy P. Williamson. *"Whatta-Gal": The Babe Didrikson Story*. Boston: Little, Brown, 1977.

Kirsch, George B. *The Creation of American Team Sports: Baseball and Cricket, 1838–72*. Urbana: University of Illinois Press, 1989.

Levine, Peter. *A. G. Spalding and the Rise of Baseball*. New York: Oxford University Press, 1989.

Mead, Chris. *Champion: Joe Lewis, Black Hero in White America*. New York: Scribners, 1985.

———. *Papa Jack: Jack Johnson and the Era of White Hopes*. New York: Free Press, 1983.

Metcalf, Alan. *Canada Learns to Play: The Emergence of Organized Sport, 1807–1914*. Toronto: McClelland & Stewart, 1987.

Midwinter, Eric. *W. G. Grace*. London: Allen & Unwin, 1981.

Naismith, James B. *Basketball: Its Origins and Development*. Reprint, Lincoln: University of Nebraska Press, 1996.

Peterson, Robert W. *Cages to Jump Shots: Pro Basketball's Early Years*. New York, Oxford University Press, 1990.

Rader, Benjamin G. *Baseball: A History of America's Game*. Urbana: University of Illinois Press, 1992.

Rader, Benjamin G. *In Its Own Image: How Television Has Transformed Sport*. New York: Free Press, 1984.

Roberts, Randy. *Jack Dempsey: The Manassa Mauler*. Baton Rouge: Louisana State University Press, 1979.

Roberts, Randy, and James Olson. *Winning Is the Only Thing: Sports in America Since 1945*. Baltimore, Md.: Johns Hopkins, 1989.

Rudolf, Wilma. *Wilma*. New York: New American Library, 1977.

Seymour, Harold. *Baseball*. 3 volumes. New York: Oxford University Press, 1960-1990.

Smith, Robert A. *A Social History of the Bicycle: Its Early Life and Times in America*. New York: American Heritage, 1972.

Tygiel, Jules. *Baseball's Great Experiment: Jackie Robinson and His Legacy*. New York: Oxford University Press, 1983.

Voigt, David Quentin. *American Baseball*. 3 volumes. Norman: University of Oklahoma Press, 1966–1983.

Wheeler, Robert W. *Jim Thorpe: World's Greatest Athlete*. Norman: University of Oklahoma Press, 1975.

Woodforde, John. *The Story of the Bicycle*. London: Routledge & Kegan Paul, 1970.

The Olympics

Carlson, Lewis H., and John J. Fogarty. *Tales of Gold: An Oral History of the Summer Olympic Games Told by America's Gold Medal Winners*. Chicago: Contemporary Books, 1987.

Chambliss, Daniel F. *Champions: The Making of Olympic Swimmers*. New York: William Morrow, 1988.

Espy, Richard. *The Politics of the Olympic Games*. Berkeley: University of California Press, 1979.

Graham, Cooper C. *Leni Riefenstahl and Olympia*. Metuchen, N.J.: Scarecrow Press, 1986.

Guttmann, Allen. *The Games Must Go On: Avery Brundage and the Olympic Movement*. New York: Columbia University Press, 1984.

———. *The Olympics: A History of the Modern Games*. Chicago: University of Illinois Press, 1992.

Halberstam, David. *The Amateurs*. New York: Viking, 1985.

Hulme, Derick L., Jr. *The Political Olympics: Moscow, Afghanistan, and the 1980 U.S. Boycott*. New York: Praeger, 1990.

Jackson, Roger, ed. *The Olympic Movement and the Mass Media*. Calgary: Hurford Enterprises, 1989.

Lucas, John. *The Modern Olympic Games*. Cranbury, N.J.: A. S. Barnes, 1980.

MacAloon, John J. *The Great Symbol: Pierre de Coubertin and the Origins of the Modern Olympic Games*. Chicago: University of Chicago Press, 1981.

Mandell, Richard D. *The Nazi Olympics*. New York: Macmillan, 1971.

———. *The First Modern Olympics*. Berkeley: University of California Press, 1976.

Reich, Kenneth. *Making It Happen: Peter Ueberroth and the 1984 Olympics*. Santa Barbara, Calif.: Capra Press, 1986.

Schaap, Dick. *Illustrated History of the Olympics*. 3rd. ed. New York: Knopf, 1975.

Simson, Vyv, and Andrew Jennings. *The Lord of the Rings: Power, Money and Drugs in the Modern Olympics*. London: Simon & Schuster, 1992.

Index

References to illustrations are indicated by page numbers in *italics*.

United States
  colonial, 41, 46–48, 64–65, 79
  frontier, 48–50
United States Olympic Committee
  (USOC), 119, 123, 124–25
Uruguay, 64

Van Wyck, Frederick, 50–51
Vanderbilt, William K., 79
Vardon, Harry, 80, 81
Velodromes, 76
Venezuela, 90
Vietnam, 16, 69
Volleyball, *87,* 111

Waitz, Grete, 10
Walker Cup, 80
Warner, Pop, *103,* 177
Water polo, 84–*85,* 125
Weatherby, James, 44–45
Webb, Matthew, 85
Weissmuller, Johnny, *85*
West Africa, 23
West Indies, 60–*61*
Western civilization, 41, 46
Wide World of Sports, 100
Wills, Helen, 78
Wingfield, Walter Clopton, 77
Women athletes. *See* Female athletes.
Works Progress Administration (WPA),
  83
World Cup, 64, 114
World Series, 94–95, 96
World War I, 106
World War II, 83, 97, 98, 100, 105,
  109, 118
Wrestling, 18–*19,* 20, 21, 23, 24, 25,
  28, 30, 31, 35, 37, 44

Young Men's Christian Association
  (YMCA), 84, 85, *87,* 106, 107, 108,
  113
Young Women's Christian Association
  (YWCA), *87*
Yuan Dynasty, 17, *18*

Zaire, 69
Zatopek, Emil, *120*
Ziert, Paul, 124

Picture Credits

About the Author

David G. McComb is professor of history at Colorado State University, where he teaches sports history. He holds an M.A. from Rice University, an M.B.A. from Stanford University, and a Ph.D. from the University of Texas at Austin. He is the author of more than 100 articles and several books, including *Texas: An Illustrated History* (Oxford University Press, 1995). He competed in age-group swimming in junior high school, high school, college, and at the master's level, cementing his life-long interest in sports—both as a participant and a spectator. Like many of us, David McComb reads the sports pages first.